Best Places to Bird
in Ontario

LOCAL EXPERTS
INSIDER KNOWLEDGE
HARD-TO-FIND BIRDS

Kenneth Burrell & **Michael Burrell**

Series editors: Russell Cannings & Richard Cannings

BEST PLACES TO BIRD IN ONTARIO

GREYSTONE BOOKS

Vancouver/Berkeley

Greystone Books Ltd.
greystonebooks.com

Cataloguing data available from Library and Archives Canada
ISBN 978-1-77164-364-1 (pbk.)
ISBN 978-1-77164-365-8 (epub)

Series editors: Russell Cannings and Richard Cannings
Editing by Lucy Kenward
Copyediting by Alison Jacques
Cover and text design by Naomi MacDougall
Cover photograph by Shutterstock/Stubblefield Photography
Maps by Eric Leinberger
Printed and bound in Canada on ancient-forest-friendly paper by Marquis

Greystone Books gratefully acknowledges the Musqueam, Squamish,
and Tsleil-Waututh peoples on whose land our office is located.

Greystone Books thanks the Canada Council for the Arts, the British Columbia
Arts Council, the Province of British Columbia through the Book Publishing Tax
Credit, and the Government of Canada for supporting our publishing activities.

Canadä

BRITISH COLUMBIA

BRITISH COLUMBIA
ARTS COUNCIL
An agency of the Province of British Columbia

Canada Council   Conseil des arts
for the Arts   du Canada

PHOTO ON PREVIOUS
SPREAD: Easily one of the
most charming species
in Ontario is the Yellow
Warbler—its arrival in spring
always signals that the other
warblers aren't too far behind.
MICHAEL BURRELL

To our parents
Without your ever-present encouragement and willingness to support us (not to mention driving us around to all of these sites as kids!), this book would not have been possible.

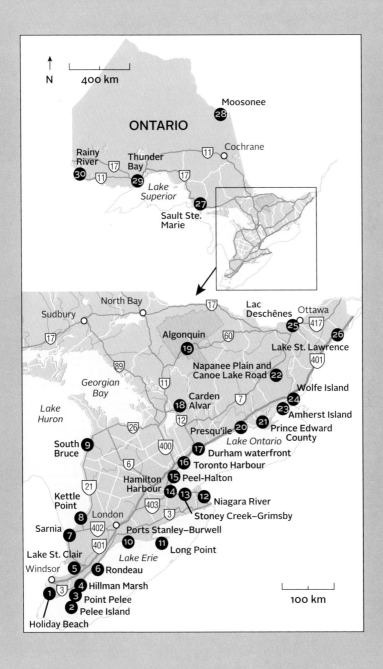

CONTENTS

INTRODUCTION

LOCATED ALONG BOTH the Atlantic and Mississippi flyways, Ontario is a birding mecca. Its diverse geography allows birders to explore the Great Lakes, the Arctic coastlines of James and Hudson Bays, expansive boreal forests, and a taste of southern Carolinian forests. The province has one of the most active birding communities on the continent and a species list approaching 500, so it's no wonder so many birders enjoy Ontario in all of its seasons.

Our own interest in birds took off one spring when our parents—who are avid birders—drove us down to Long Point to drop off a few dozen Prothonotary Warbler nest boxes. We were pre-teens at the time, and as we met the wonderful people of Bird Studies Canada, attended the Doug Tarry Young Ornithologists' Workshop, and realized how lucky we were to live in such an ecologically and ornithologically rich region, we also became aware that birding was an actual career path we could pursue. Since then, both of us have been absolutely obsessed with birds and we've spent most of our free time learning and chasing birds from one corner of the province to the next.

Both of us had talked about sharing our knowledge of Ontario birds in book form at some point, so when the opportunity presented itself, we knew we couldn't pass it up—even knowing we were in for some late nights of pulling together all the bits of knowledge we had gained over two decades of birding.

We knew that we wanted to make this book different from Clive Goodwin's *A Bird-Finding Guide to Ontario*, published in 1995. And it soon became apparent that it would be a fair bit different, primarily in that it covers our favourite sites in more depth, including updated information on the sites and birds themselves, birding strategies, and natural and cultural history sprinkled with some personal stories.

At first, formulating a list of the top 30 places to bird in the province sounds easy, but we quickly found that isn't the case. We didn't apply a rigorous scientific method to the task; rather, each of us started with our top five areas to bird, and from there we added other favourites. Making the list was easy; whittling it down to 30 was not! The list of top birding destinations in Ontario is extensive.

In making our final selection, we tried to find a balance of locations across the province and in different ecological zones. We also took into account where most of our readers would be, considering both visiting birders and birders who live in the province, which is why we have included many areas within a couple of hours of the Greater Toronto Area (GTA). Ultimately, we are happy with the sites we have chosen, but we know that not everyone will agree with our choices. We just didn't have space for some of the other excellent birding spots, including the Hudson Bay coastline, Haldimand County, the upper Bruce, Manitoulin Island, the north shore of Lake Superior, and Luther Marsh, to name a few.

You may also notice some personal biases in the book, notably that the Kingston and Pelee areas are thoroughly covered. Mike lived for two years in Kingston, and Ken spent entire springs down at Pelee doing research for his master's thesis, which means we have lots of in-depth knowledge that we really felt we should share. In every chapter, we have tried to provide detailed information that will be useful for birders of all skill levels, whether living in the area or travelling through. Included for each location is a site overview, a birding guide to the area with helpful tips, and directions to get there.

FINDING THE BIRDS

If you haven't joined eBird (ebird.ca), do so before you set out. eBird provides birders around the world with a host of information, such as latest sightings and interactive range maps, and in Ontario a large proportion of birders use it to log their sightings. As such, via eBird you have access to up-to-date information about what birds are being seen and where.

The Ontario Field Ornithologists (OFO) (ofo.ca) is the leading organization for birders in the province. The OFO organizes field trips throughout the year all over the province; runs the Ontbirds listserv, which disseminates information about rare bird sightings in Ontario; and produces an excellent newsletter (*OFO News*) and journal (*Ontario Birds*) tailored to birding in the province (both published three times a year). We feel strongly that all Ontario birders should be members.

BIRDING ETHICS

Anyone who spends their time searching out birds is bound to also want to protect them and preserve their habitat. The OFO has a code of ethics for all those who observe or photograph birds, and we feel strongly that the following principles from the code are most noteworthy:

Keep disturbance to a minimum.

Always assume that a bird is sensitive to your presence. Although some birds can tolerate human activity, this varies from species to species and from season to season.

To avoid stressing birds or exposing birds to danger, exercise restraint during observation, photography, sound recording, or filming.

Do not deliberately flush birds.

Limit the use of [audio] playbacks or other methods of attracting birds. Never use such methods in heavily birded areas, or for attracting any species that is Endangered, Threatened, or of Special Concern, or is rare in your local area.

Do not trespass. Always obtain permission to enter sites that are posted.

We can't stress what's stated above enough, particularly when viewing rare or at-risk species and owls.

BIRDING IN ONTARIO

For birders visiting Ontario, there are a few things to be aware of when out and about.

Ticks. Ticks carrying Lyme disease are now fairly regular in much of southern Ontario, so taking precautions such as tucking your pants into your socks and doing daily tick checks is a good idea. Mosquitoes and other biting flies (black flies and deer flies, mainly) can also be a major irritant; mosquitoes generally peak in June, black flies in late May, and deer flies in July. When visiting any wooded habitats in June, you'll likely want to wear a long-sleeved shirt and bring bug spray.

Seasonal weather. If you're birding in spring or fall migration, you'll want to pay close attention to the weather. In spring migration, birds typically arrive following a warm front with winds from the south that bring the warmer temperatures. Conversely, in fall, birds arrive following a cold front with winds from the north that bring the cooler temperatures. In both cases, if you can get these conditions at night interrupted by inclement weather (e.g., rain, high winds, thunder/lightning), you have the right conditions for a large "grounding" or "fallout" of birds. As such, the best days for birding at these times of year often involve some precipitation.

In winter, be aware that winter storms are not infrequent, especially near the Great Lakes, which can produce "lake-effect" snow squalls that are highly intense and sometimes surprisingly concentrated. At that time of year, come prepared with warm clothing and boots and a vehicle equipped with snow tires. (Most rental car companies don't provide snow tires as a standard option, so you may want to inquire about this add-on as it makes a big difference when driving on snow.)

Traffic. Another consideration is the size of the province. Don't be fooled: getting from one end of Ontario to the other can take a full day or more of driving. The major highways are generally in good condition and traffic moves at a good speed, but travel through the GTA can be extremely slow with heavy traffic. There is a toll highway (Hwy. 407) that offers an "express" route along the north edge of the GTA, but it can cost upward of $40 a trip. Winter travel can also be slow anywhere, especially during snowstorms, so leave extra time.

1

HOLIDAY BEACH AND LOWER DETROIT RIVER

OVERVIEW

A relatively small, yet highly diverse area (over 300 species have been found here), this region of southwestern Ontario covers two distinct Important Bird and Biodiversity Areas (IBAs): Holiday Beach Conservation Area and the Lower Detroit River. These areas have been designated as IBAs for drastically different reasons and they support fairly different birdlife.

The Lower Detroit River is a waterbird mecca. In fall and throughout the winter, the river is home to more than 1% of the global population of Canvasbacks and more than 1% of the

◀ Those "dots" you see way up in the sky are actually birds—thousands of Broad-winged Hawks like the ones pictured here migrate along the shoreline in spectacular numbers each fall. JOSH BOUMAN

North American population of Common Mergansers, with annual counts exceeding 14,000 and 7,000, respectively. In the past, the area hosted one of the largest Ring-billed Gull colonies in the world, though they disappeared rather suddenly a few years ago—hopefully they will return. Smaller numbers of Common Terns nest here as well, though in nowhere near the numbers found historically.

Holiday Beach complements the fine waterbirding along the Lower Detroit River because it lies on the flight path for many migrating birds. Since crossing large bodies of water poses a major risk to many birds, a lot of them will try their best to avoid doing so. As birds are flying south in the fall to get to their wintering grounds, Holiday Beach's position at the southwestern corner of Ontario is essentially at the bottom of a giant bird funnel formed by the Great Lakes and the Detroit River. At that time of year, you get a spectacle not seen at many other inland locations in the world: a virtual "river of raptors." Globally significant numbers of Broad-winged Hawks (over 100,000), Sharp-shinned Hawks (over 18,000), and Turkey Vultures (over 50,000) migrate through between September and mid-November. If you like Blue Jays and American Goldfinches too, chances are you'll get your fill of them, with average annual counts exceeding 300,000 and 25,000. If those weren't reason enough to visit, a few pairs of Prothonotary Warblers and a great assortment of marsh birds nest here, providing a complete birding package throughout the year.

BIRDING STRATEGY
Starting at the intersection of Essex County Road (CR) 50 and Lake Erie Country Club Dr., take Lake Erie Country Club

Dr. south to the end of the road. Checking for birds in the marsh alongside this road is a must; it offers a great assortment of marsh-bird species, with Common Gallinule, Great Egret, Black-crowned Night-Heron, Forster's Tern, and the ubiquitous Mute Swan present from mid-April to early fall. In spring and fall migration, the forested stands closer to the lake can be good for songbirds, while in winter, the sheltered areas here can harbour late migrants and scarce over-winterers, such as the odd Common Yellowthroat and Marsh Wren. The marsh connects directly with Holiday Beach Conservation Area, which is just a stone's throw away to the west.

To get there, return to Essex CR 50 and turn west (left) for 500 m/yds. Note that a small fee is required at the pay station to enter Holiday Beach Conservation Area. After a few hundred metres, you'll cross the channel that runs across Lake Erie Country Club Dr. to the east. Here you'll spot the same species as along Lake Erie Country Club Dr. as well as having a view of the large marsh to your west. Continuing into the conservation area brings you to the seasonal camping area. In migration, walk throughout this area and the trails between here and the marsh to see songbirds on par with any of the migrant hotspots along Lake Erie, such as Point Pelee (Chapter 3) and Rondeau Provincial Park (Chapter 6). In May, you can often find a dozen species of warbler and close to half a dozen flycatcher and vireo species. Continue driving/walking along the main road farther into the conservation area; you'll notice signs for endangered breeding species. A few pairs of Prothonotary Warblers have nested here in recent years; they favour the swampy habitats along the marsh periphery.

Once you've gone as far as you can on the main road, stay to the right to reach the observation tower. It provides a

360-degree view of the area, specifically of the marsh to the north and west, and in autumn is a great way to take in hawks in flight. Here, the Holiday Beach Migration Observatory, in conjunction with the Essex Region Conservation Authority, runs the Festival of Hawks on the second and third weekends of September. A hawk counter is present every day during fall migration (early September to late November) and is a great resource to ask about recent sightings. Generally speaking, the best days for raptor migration are days following strong cold fronts that bring northwest winds and a bit of cloud cover. Birders can expect to find 11+ species of hawks and eagles over the course of the season, including over 100 Golden Eagles and the odd Swainson's Hawk, along with the more common Ontario raptors.

If you aren't too busy looking at raptors overhead, the tower provides a great vantage to scope the marsh. Over the years this location has recorded a major list of rarities, including Purple Gallinule, Vermilion Flycatcher, Glossy and White-faced Ibises, and Little Blue Heron, to name a few. The tower is also a great spot for keen observers to try their luck (and patience) with identifying songbirds in flight in the fall, not to mention plenty of herons, ducks, and grebes throughout the marsh.

Once you've covered Holiday Beach, head back to Essex CR 50. Take this west (left) to the small hamlet of Malden Centre. At the intersection, turn west (left) onto Essex CR 20 and continue until you reach the bridge that spans Big Creek. The bridge provides a good viewing location of the large wetland that feeds into Holiday Beach and is a great spot for herons and egrets, with the occasional rare southern heron also showing up. Usually a few Purple Martins and Forster's Terns are here in the summer, along with the odd Bald Eagle.

From the bridge over Big Creek, continue west on Essex CR 20 to Glen Eden and turn left (south) onto Front Rd. South. At McLeod Ave., turn left (east) and in 300 m/yds turn left (north) again to park in the small lot at Warren Mickle Park. This parking lot also serves as the starting point for the Amherstburg Birding and Nature Trail, an easy 5.25 km (3.3 mi.) loop that mostly follows quiet roads through marsh and wooded areas. The best areas for birding are in the wooded section along the shoreline and the Bar Point Marsh, a few hundred metres east of the parking lot. The trail is best during songbird migration—primarily mid-April to the end of May and again from late August through October. Walking the trail in peak migration can yield excellent diversity, with sparrows, thrushes, vireos, and warblers all being abundant on good days.

Once you've checked out the birding trail, return to your car, continue back to Essex CR 20, and follow it north, along the Detroit River. There are a number of spots to visit along the river in the late fall, in the winter, and again in the early spring—all of which can be excellent for large numbers of waterfowl and other waterbirds. Expect to see Canvasbacks, Common Mergansers, and Redheads, with lesser numbers of Bonaparte's Gulls, Common Loons, and Horned Grebes. A few pairs of Bald Eagles nest nearby and in winter there can be lots along the river. When birding the Lower Detroit River, checking several locations will yield the best results, especially since concentrations of birds move around from day to day in response to changing ice and food conditions. We generally recommend the following spots: the Boblo Island Ferry

Terminal, Alma Street lookout, Amherstburg Visitor Centre, and Angstrom Park. All are easily accessed off Essex CR 20 within 10 km (6 mi.) of the intersection with Front Rd.

While you're birding in the Holiday Beach and Lower Detroit River area, driving the back roads—particularly in the winter—can be productive for a variety of birds, notably lingering blackbirds and sparrows. In irruption years, Snowy Owls are found periodically in the large, open fields to the north and east.

GETTING THERE

The region is highly accessible from the north and east, as it's situated just 20 minutes south of Windsor along Essex CR 20, and 25 minutes west of Kingsville along Essex CR 50. For birders visiting Point Pelee, Holiday Beach is a 40-minute drive.

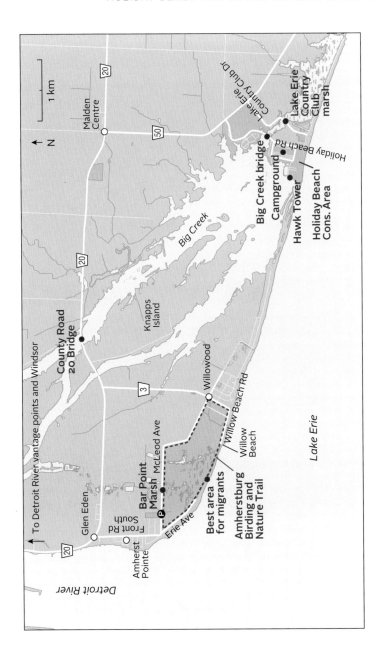

Birding (and photography!) along the west side of Fish Point in the evening can be fantastic. Scarlet Tanagers in all their brilliance shine among our favourites.

BRANDON HOLDEN

2

PELEE ISLAND

OVERVIEW

Originally a group of three small islands with an expansive marsh connecting them, the current Pelee Island was created when European settlers drained the marsh in the 1800s. Just 10 km (6 mi.) long and 4 km (2.6 mi.) wide, the island has a mild climate and a long growing season (among the longest in Canada) that supports an interesting agricultural community now best known for its vineyards and budding tourism industry. While it is located only 25 km (15.5 mi.) from Point Pelee National Park, Pelee Island is vastly underbirded in comparison with its popular neighbour, particularly in May. That said, there is considerable interest here from birders and conservationists alike.

The Pelee Island Bird Observatory (PIBO), which was formed in 2003, undertakes a migration-monitoring program during spring and fall at Fish Point Provincial Park on the island's south end. In addition, over the last decade the Nature Conservancy of Canada (NCC) has acquired land and done a tremendous amount of public engagement throughout the island, and between the NCC, Ontario Parks, the Essex Region Conservation Authority (ERCA), and Ontario Nature, over 15% of the island's land is formally protected—much of it actively being restored to natural habitat.

Birders know the island best for its spring migration, especially during the month of May; however, the island provides good birding in all seasons due largely to its geographic location (for migrant birds) and southern latitude (for rare Carolinian breeders). Fish Point and Lighthouse Point Provincial Parks are two of the top hotspots, with over 2.5 km (1.5 mi.) of hiking trails and boardwalks. Neotropic migrants (warblers, vireos, flycatchers, etc.) pass through the island in sometimes mind-boggling numbers, especially in May and September when the number of different species is also at its peak. Warblers are definitely the crowd pleasers, with up to 30 species being seen on a single day during peak migration. Southern rarities like Summer Tanagers, Blue Grosbeaks, and Kentucky and Yellow-throated Warblers are seen annually. Fall throughout the island is a less rushed affair, with migrants starting to pass through in earnest in late August. Mid-September is the peak, with days following strong cold fronts and north winds being the best.

The breeding season (June and July) is a quieter (and hotter) time of year. Several nationally rare species, such as Prothonotary Warbler and Yellow-breasted Chat, are known to breed on the island. Many of the regenerating properties now preserved by NCC and ERCA are frequented by old-field species, such as Orchard Orioles, Eastern Towhees, Indigo

Buntings, and lots of Yellow Warblers. Herons (Great Blue Herons, Black-crowned Night-Herons, and Great Egrets, typically) are also present in generally high numbers, as birds from nesting colonies on the adjacent islands come to Pelee Island to feed. Lastly, the long sand spit at Fish Point is a great place to check at any time of the year for gulls and terns, as well as other waterbirds.

Winter is generally mild because the island is moderated by the waters of Lake Erie, and good numbers of sparrows are usually present in the brushy areas, including uncommon winterers such as Chipping and Field Sparrows and Eastern Towhees. You can usually see large concentrations of ducks offshore, with Red-breasted Mergansers, Buffleheads, and Common Goldeneyes being most abundant. Other waterbirds, such as Common Loons, Horned Grebes, and Bonaparte's Gulls, are also present in good numbers.

BIRDING STRATEGY
During migration, it's best to pay close attention to the weather and to bird the lee side of the island. Walking or cycling along public roads is a great way to see birds, and areas around woodlots and wooded canals are particularly good during migration.

Starting at Fish Point Provincial Park, walk the central path out to the southern tip of the island. Along the way, check Fox Pond, about 300 m/yds from the parking lot, for Wood Ducks and any herons in the area. Take your time continuing to the tip; the woods throughout are great for migrant warblers and orioles. Once at the tip, check for birds resting on the spit; first and last light are often the best times to visit, especially to find vagrants that are stopping only briefly. In spring migration, and particularly on days with southerly winds, a reorientation flight—a morning flight of songbirds heading south (!) over the lake—often occurs during the first few hours of the day. Watching songbirds stream south off the tip can be a good way to spot rare species; however, identifying these small birds in flight can be a challenge. We've generally found that when there are few birds at the point, it's best to cut your losses and move on. You can walk back the way you came or stroll along the west beach (which is especially good on days with east winds or calm evenings). Back at the parking lot, heading west along McCormick Rd. towards Mosquito Point can yield more migrants, and a pair of Prothonotary Warblers has nested in recent years in the wet slough on the north side of the road.

Continuing north along McCormick Rd., keep an eye on the lake for waterbirds: Horned Grebes are regularly seen in migration, as well as Buffleheads and Bonaparte's Gulls. As you continue north, you'll come to a stop sign at the intersection of East West Rd. Turn right (east) and drive a few hundred metres. Immediately following the Masonic Lodge, there's a trail entrance to the Pelee Island Winery's interpretive nature trail on your right (south). The trails here can be good during migration, and White-eyed Vireos have nested in recent years.

Heading east along the East West Rd., you'll reach Stone Rd. and the famous Stone Road Alvar to the south. Trails on both sides of Stone Rd. lead into the alvar, which is one of the best places to see nesting Yellow-breasted Chats not only on Pelee Island but in all of Ontario. Listen for the chat's raucous calls in the late evening or early morning in June and early July. Eastern Towhees and Field Sparrows are common breeders, while the shrubby woods can be attractive for migrants during spring and fall. In spring, the alvar can be very wet, so birding from the road may be preferable.

Continue north from the alvar, and catch East Shore Rd. to travel north up the east side of the island. Birding the wooded canals on foot along this road and Lorain Lane to the north can be very productive, especially on days with west winds. Get back in your car and when you reach the intersection with Brown's Rd. a few kilometres north, stop. Park on the side of the road, and go for a walk in the woods to the south and east of this location. This area is known as Brown's Woods, or Middle Point. There aren't any trails; however, NCC allows visitors and you can walk along either the road or the beach. If you venture off the beach or the road, be aware that Poison Ivy is abundant! The woods here are among our favourites, with virtually all of the "regular" southern warblers (Kentucky, Prothonotary, Worm-eating) being seen here in migration. Great Horned and Eastern Screech-Owls are common year-round, while the woods have your typical southern Ontario woodland nesting birds, including Red-eyed Vireos and Rose-breasted Grosbeaks.

North of Middle Point, continue until the road ends at Lighthouse Point Provincial Park. The parking area is about 200 m/yds south of the end of the road. There's a small trail only a few hundred metres in total that leads north from the dead end through dense shrub, runs along the beach, and ends at the lighthouse. The trail here can be absolutely spectacular during migration; most years it attracts virtually all of the regular neotropic migrants expected in Ontario. The "bowl" immediately west of the lighthouse is a favourite of ours and has turned up some good birds in the past, like Yellow-throated and Cerulean Warblers. Lighting is best in the morning.

As you're leaving Lighthouse Point, Lake Henry on your right (west) is a great spot for herons and egrets, as well as dabbling ducks in spring and fall. During periods of strong winds, this is a good spot to check for waterbirds riding out the inclement weather. Red-breasted Mergansers, Horned Grebes, and the odd Ruddy Duck can be seen on the lake in migration.

From Lighthouse Point, continue west along the north shore, following Harris Garno Rd., Scudder Rd., and then the North Shore Rd. until you reach the cemetery, just past the Anchor and Wheel Inn. This is the start of Sheridan Point, and walking the roads along the forested and shrubby areas is the best strategy in migration. At the end of the road, check the breakwall for roosting shorebirds, including rare western shorebirds like Willets and Marbled Godwits as well as more common species like Ruddy Turnstones and Black-bellied Plovers. The inner water within the breakwall can also be good for wintering waterbirds, like a Harlequin Duck that was here in 2011.

Driving the interior roads of the island is the best strategy for birding in the winter. Snowy Owls can be seen during invasion years, along with Rough-legged Hawks and Northern Harriers. The soy and corn fields in winter are also good bets for flocks of Snow Buntings and Horned Larks. Looking through these flocks can turn up Lapland Longspurs and the odd Savannah Sparrow.

GETTING THERE

Pelee Island can be reached by air and by ferry. Local providers operate regular flights from Windsor during the winter months. The Owen Sound Transportation Company typically runs ferry service from Leamington or Kingsville to the island from late March/early April until mid-December, depending on ice and wind conditions, with sailings 2–3 times a day, seven days a week. Advance reservations are strongly encouraged, particularly on weekends and if you plan to bring a vehicle. Information on sailing dates and schedules is available through the Owen Sound Transportation Company's website.

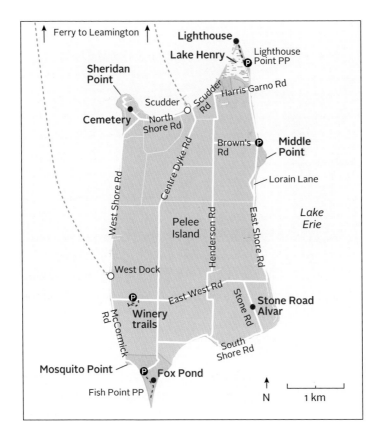

Checking patches of grass like those around the Serengeti Tree or Sparrow Field can pop up Pelee specialties, like this Henslow's Sparrow. MICHAEL BURRELL

3

POINT PELEE
NATIONAL PARK

OVERVIEW

Arguably the best place to bird in Ontario, Point Pelee is the
most southerly piece of mainland Canada and sits at the same
latitude as northern California. This sand spit, formed over
thousands of years by erosion and sedimentation, stretches
10 km (6 mi.) south into Lake Erie and its north–south axis
makes it a funnel for migrating birds in both spring and fall.
In 1918, the point was established as a national park because
of its importance for migratory birds. Point Pelee is known
among Canadian and international birders as the "warbler
capital of North America": over 40 warbler species are seen
here among the nearly 400 total species in the area.

Over the years, we've had some of our best birding days

here: fallouts in May can be so intense that warblers have literally flown between the two of us as we stood side by side. While such an abundance of migrants doesn't occur daily or even annually, spending a week here in peak spring migration should net you 1–2 "good" days.

The park is best known for its spring migration; however, birding can be great in all seasons. In fact, the fall can bring a more impressive number of birds and far fewer people. Summer offers a taste of Carolinian birding, with rare southern species like Yellow-breasted Chats and Prothonotary Warblers breeding here. In winter, due to the mild temperatures associated with the southern latitude and warm waters of Lake Erie, rare wintering species like Fox Sparrow, Yellow-rumped Warbler, and Hermit Thrush are regularly present.

Birding at Point Pelee is often combined with trips to Hillman Marsh (Chapter 4), as well as Lake St. Clair (Chapter 5), Rondeau Provincial Park (Chapter 6), and Holiday Beach (Chapter 1). Typically, we try to do this in any season. In May, we usually bird the park in the morning and early afternoon before heading north, checking the onion fields as well as Hillman Marsh and Wheatley, and occasionally going all the way to Lake St. Clair.

The park itself is relatively small and all of the trails within it can easily be covered over the course of 2–3 days. A small fee, paid to the attendant at the park gate, is required to gain entry. The park is open year-round, generally from sunrise to sunset in winter, and earlier/later, particularly in May, when the park is inundated with thousands of visiting birders.

Similar in many ways to places like Pelee Island, Rondeau, and Long Point, Point Pelee is well known for neotropic migrants passing through in spring and fall. The park is a

Soaking in the view at the tip of Point Pelee each morning is one of the most enjoyable things we do each May. This is also "the" spot to watch for birds reorienting in the first few hours of the day. BRANDON HOLDEN

magnet for rare birds, with vagrants from all over the continent showing up. In spring, southern overshoots—species such as Worm-eating and Kentucky Warblers, Summer Tanagers, Blue Grosbeaks that "overshoot" their normal range assisted by warm, southerly spring winds—are especially known to show up here. Like Fish Point on Pelee Island, the tip of Point Pelee regularly has "reverse migration" events, where songbirds fly south over the open water in the first few hours, offering intrepid birders a chance to identify birds in flight.

Birding here in the summer can be particularly hot and humid; however, early to mid-June is best for breeding species and some very rare migrants have also shown up at this time of year. White-eyed Vireos, Prothonotary Warblers, and

Yellow-breasted Chats have bred here recently, and the park is the best place in the province to find breeding Orchard Orioles. Species like Eastern Wood-Pewee, American Redstart, and Red-eyed Vireo are common in the wooded areas, and Field Sparrow, Eastern Towhee, and Yellow Warbler are present in the open areas.

In fall and early winter and spring, waterbird concentrations can be excellent; thousands of waterfowl are present, primarily Red-breasted Merganser, all three scoters, Greater Scaup, and Common Goldeneye. Loons, grebes, and gulls are typically here in good numbers too, and on days with strong southwest winds, watching the lake from the tip of Point Pelee can yield excellent numbers and variety of waterbirds.

BIRDING STRATEGY

We almost always start our day at the tip of Point Pelee—even on days we expect the birding there to be slow, because as Forrest Gump said, "You never know what you're gonna get." Bringing a scope is highly recommended, as waterbirds are typically far offshore. Watch the tip for a few minutes: especially at sunrise you'll see birds moving by and throughout the day you'll find them foraging.

Pay particular attention to the weather conditions. We always try to bird the lee side of the point, where it's sheltered and theoretically there should be more insects and therefore more birds. Walking north from the tip, on the west side we check the area known as the Serengeti Tree, the only large Honey Locust tree in the area, which is roughly 150 m/yds north of the tram drop-off area. In late April and early May, the grassy area around the tree is a favourite spot for rare sparrows, like Henslow's and LeConte's. Opposite the Serengeti

Tree, on the east side of the point, lies the Sparrow Field, another great spot for sparrows, as well as for birds foraging along the forest edge, like Yellow-breasted Chat and White-eyed Vireo. Checking the lake on the east side can also be productive for waterbirds, particularly on west winds, when the lake is sheltered here.

Walking north from the Sparrow Field and Serengeti Tree, you have three options. Walk the west beach, the main road, or a seasonal footpath through Post Woods that connects to Woodland Nature Trail (WNT); all will lead you back to the Visitor Centre (VC) and can be excellent. The west beach provides good vantage points for scanning the lake in all seasons and has attracted Kirtland's Warblers in recent years. Orchard Orioles are plentiful here (and everywhere else in the park), while sparrows like the open shrub habitats, and diurnal migrants can often be detected flying overhead. The paved road provides steady birding in migration, particularly on windy days. During peak migration 15–20 species of warblers can regularly be seen in this area. The Post Woods trail is equally good, particularly the area just north of the Sparrow Field, where we've had good luck seeing Connecticut and Cerulean Warblers in recent springs.

After you've checked these options, two trails are located around the VC: the WNT, and the Tilden Woods and Shuster Trail. These are two of the most reliable sites in the park during migration: they regularly have dozens of warblers—Blackburnian, Mourning, Canada, Hooded, Blue-winged, and Bay-breasted—to whet your appetite, as well as all of the rarer warblers over the course of a spring. If the park is quiet, try the wooded sloughs, as birds seem to be attracted to the water. While it's easy to leave the VC as quickly as you came, the parking lot offers a clear view of the sky to watch for diurnal migrants overhead and has had its fair share of rarities over the years, including Black Swift, Neotropic Cormorant, both Mississippi and Swallow-tailed Kites, and many more. Keep an eye up, particularly on days with north or northeast winds, as birds will follow the point as they move southwest along the Lake Erie shoreline. This is true in both spring and fall migrations.

Moving north from the VC, the Cactus Field, cemetery, and DeLaurier Homestead and associated trails can be excellent for migrants, particularly old-field species. In summer, watch for Black Terns over the marsh from the DeLaurier Trail. Until fairly recently, Yellow-breasted Chats nested regularly along Anders Footpath between DeLaurier Homestead and the cemetery, so be aware of their strange series of calls. At dusk, the area around the homestead is a fan favourite for observing displays of American Woodcock in April and May.

Along the west shore from the VC and north to the park gate sit eight picnic shelters (West Beach, White Pine, Black Willow, Pioneer, Sleepy Hollow, Dunes, Northwest Beach, and Sanctuary). Connecting these picnic shelters are several seasonal birding trails and the Centennial Bike and Hike Trail. Walking these areas is great on windy days or if you want to get away from crowds of birders in the spring. These spots are among our personal favourites and routinely produce Hooded, Prairie, Cerulean, and Golden-winged Warblers among the other more common species. Checking the lake for waterbirds is always worthwhile, and the same goes for the beach grass for sparrows. Looking under pieces of driftwood can sometimes yield Five-lined Skinks, and the area can also be good for migrant butterflies.

Opposite Northwest Beach is the Marsh Boardwalk—a favourite spot to lunch and to take a quick stroll in the evening. The boardwalk is an easy walk and a good place to observe marsh species that few other spots in the park provide. Swamp Sparrows, both American and Least Bitterns, Black Terns, and Soras breed here. Dawn or dusk is typically the best time to check for these species, when they're most active. An observation tower at the beginning of the trail provides a good vantage point over the marsh. Visitors can rent kayaks and canoes from the park store here and bird the marsh by boat, especially in late summer and early fall, when there can be shorebird habitat in the far reaches.

Heading north out of the park, take the first road—Mersea Rd. E. The road runs east along the canal that forms the boundary of the park, and we like to drive slowly along this road with our windows open. The dyke is largely overgrown with shrubs and trees and is an overlooked spot for migrants as well as waterbirds using the canal itself. The agricultural fields between here and Leamington and Hillman Marsh are known to birders as "the onion fields"—driving the roads through this area can be very productive for shorebirds and waterfowl during migration.

GETTING THERE

Point Pelee National Park is easily accessed by car. The park is 3.5 hours from Toronto and 3 hours from Hamilton and Kitchener-Waterloo. Hwy. 401 provides the quickest route here; take exit 48, for Comber. Follow Hwy. 77/Comber Sideroad (SR) south to Leamington. Driving south through Leamington along Hwy. 77, the road becomes Erie St. S; take this through Leamington to the intersection with Seacliff

Dr./Essex Rd. 20. Head east on Seacliff Dr. E about 1 km (0.6 mi.) until you come to the Y intersection with Bevel Line Rd./Essex Rd. 33. Turn right onto Bevel Line Rd./Essex Rd. 33 and continue for about 5 km (3 mi.) until you reach the park gate.

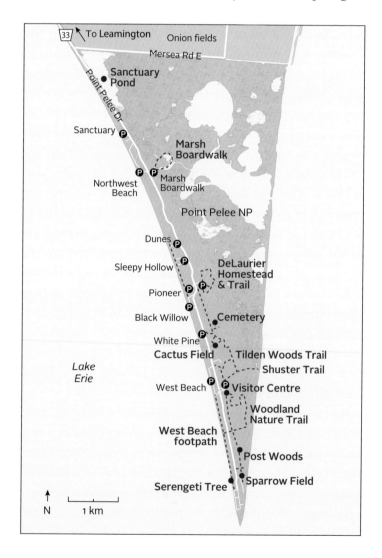

4
HILLMAN MARSH AND WHEATLEY

OVERVIEW

Hillman Marsh and the neighbouring town of Wheatley should be on the list of any birder in the province: over 300 species have been recorded in this small area alone! The list of exceptional rarities found here over the years is staggering: Kelp(!), Slaty-backed, and Ivory Gulls, just about every rare heron/ibis, Neotropic Cormorant, Brown Pelican, Swallow-tailed Kite, Gray Kingbird . . . the list just keeps going.

Formerly known as Stein's Marsh, Hillman Marsh is operated by the Essex Region Conservation Authority (ERCA) and is one of the few remaining lakeshore wetlands in extreme southwestern Ontario. The marsh consists of a shorebird lagoon (the "shorebird cell"), a small regenerating woodland and prairie, and an expansive marsh that flows into Lake Erie.

North of the marsh is the town of Wheatley, one of the last commercial fisheries along Lake Erie. Of interest to birders within the town of Wheatley are the harbour, the provincial park, and Campers Cove Rd. To maximize our day when birding here, we typically visit Point Pelee National Park (Chapter 3) in the morning, followed by Hillman Marsh and the Wheatley area in the afternoon/early evening. This approach is particularly good in the spring.

At Hillman, the shorebird cell is an excellent place to spot migrant waterfowl and shorebirds in the spring, including globally significant numbers of Black-bellied Plovers passing through in mid-to-late May. The number and diversity of shorebirds generally peak around the Victoria Day long weekend. Ducks, herons, and gulls are also seen here in excellent numbers, not to mention songbirds within the shrubby woodland habitats bordering the cell. The marsh itself is a great location for wetland species, such as American Coots, Wood Ducks, Great Egrets, and rails. A small entrance fee (payable at the gatehouse) is required to enter the marsh; however, we'd recommend buying an annual pass (which can be purchased at the gatehouse if there is an attendant on duty or online at ERCA's website), as it's definitely a spot you'll want to check many times while in the area.

Wheatley Harbour is another excellent location, just a few kilometres from Hillman Marsh. It's always worth a look, and stops can be quite quick and easy. The harbour is generally least productive in the summer, though it has produced some of the best vagrants in the province at this time of year. Gulls typically loaf on the breakwalls waiting for fishing boats to bring in their catch, while shorebirds—generally present from late April through early October—frequent the beach.

The shorebird cell at Hillman Marsh is the province's best spot for American Avocets (background) and Willets (foreground) during their northward migrations. BRANDON HOLDEN

Wheatley Provincial Park is another great migrant trap, and while it is underbirded compared to Point Pelee National Park, it boasts a similarly impressive list of species. Near the park is Campers Cove Rd., the most reliable place in Ontario in the last decade for breeding Dickcissels.

From late February to the end of April is prime waterfowl migration, with thousands of ducks and sometimes even more Tundra Swans frequenting the area. Large warm fronts, particularly in late February and early March, can bring flocks of Greater White-fronted and Snow Geese along with smaller numbers of Ross's Geese to Hillman Marsh and the surrounding fields. As the season progresses, flocks of several thousand Redheads typically show up in mid-to-late March, followed by the first Blue-winged and Green-winged Teals in early April.

As May approaches, shorebirds start to arrive, with the cell and the beach at Wheatley Harbour being by far the best places to check. Herons and ducks are good bets at Hillman, while Wheatley Harbour is a great place to look for gulls attracted by the fishing boats.

Summer is generally slower; however, Hillman Marsh is a great place for marsh breeders. Least Bittern, Sora, Marsh Wren, and Swamp Sparrow are all regular here, and King Rails are probably here most years, though hard to find. As fall begins to pick up, the cell can be good for shorebirds if the water levels are appropriate. Late fall can be especially good at the harbour too, with jaegers, and interesting shorebirds like Red Phalarope and Purple Sandpiper, being seen occasionally.

Overall, both locations can be excellent at all times of the year, though we'd recommend checking during the spring (March to May) and fall (August to November) migrations.

BIRDING STRATEGY

There are essentially three main areas to check while at Hillman Marsh and Wheatley: the cell, the marsh trail, and the town of Wheatley. All can be especially productive depending on the time of year and the weather conditions.

From the main parking lot at Hillman Marsh (adjacent to Hillman United Church), walk the trail to the south towards the cell. Keep an ear out for the loud call of the Ring-necked Pheasant at all times of the year. Once at the cell, it's generally easiest to scan the flats from the T-junction where the trail intersects the dyke surrounding the cell, or from the shorebird-viewing platform to your southeast (you'll be able to see it). While walking along the dyke, be diligent in trying not to scare any birds; moving slowly, you should be able to get quite close to them without trouble. In the evenings, it's often worth scanning the cell from the west or south side (opposite the shorebird blind) as the lighting will be better. The brushy areas along the edge of the cell can be good in migration for warblers and other migrants too.

During spring shorebirding season, it's generally best to bird here in the afternoon if you're short on time, as that's when birds migrating from the Chesapeake Bay area start to arrive. The cell has had over 35 species of shorebirds, and in recent years Black-necked Stilt, Ruff, and Curlew Sandpiper have been spotted. The cell is easily southern Ontario's best location for seeing American Avocet, Willet, and Marbled Godwit. While these are generally rare or uncommon species, Dunlin, Black-bellied and Semipalmated Plovers, and Short-billed Dowitcher are common.

After you've checked the cell, walking the marsh trail to

the northeast can be productive for wetland species. Winter can turn up unexpected lingerers, such as Common Yellowthroat and Marsh Wren. During the spring and summer, Least Bitterns are present in small numbers, and in some years King Rails breed, though less so in recent years. Try listening for rails in the evening. Walking the trails in the early morning in fall can occasionally turn up species like Nelson's Sparrow, while good numbers of warblers and sparrows can be seen reliably too. During years of low water levels, the marsh will occasionally form large mud flats. If this is the case, incredible numbers of shorebirds can be present from late July to mid-October.

Leave Hillman Marsh and drive north to the town of Wheatley by taking Mersea Rd. 2 east. Turn left (north) onto Mersea Rd. 21 for one concession before turning right (east) onto Fox Run Rd. While on Mersea Rd. 21 and Fox Run Rd., keep an eye on the fields—they regularly flood in spring and can be excellent for shorebirds and waterfowl. In 2014, they even hosted a group of Smith's Longspurs! Once on Fox Run Rd., turn left (north) at the lake onto Pulley Rd., where you'll parallel the lakeshore for a kilometre before turning left onto Milo Rd. Once you're on Milo Rd., Wheatley Harbour will be on your right after a few hundred metres.

The harbour can be hit or miss; however, it's always worth checking because it takes only five minutes, which means you aren't wasting much time if it's a bust. Gulls will loaf on the breakwalls and/or beach: 18 species of gulls have been seen here! Shorebirds will also roost on the breakwall and beach, and both spots can be checked thoroughly and efficiently. You can scan the harbour from either the west or east side, but the beach is visible only from the east. If you care about these things, be aware that the county line between Chatham-Kent and Essex runs approximately down the middle of the harbour. At the north end of the harbour is Muddy Creek, which is another easy spot to check that is very reliable for Green Heron and Great Egret and has hosted several rare herons and Neotropic Cormorants over the years.

At the northeast corner of town is Wheatley Provincial Park (accessed off Klondyke Rd.). An entrance fee (payable at the pay station) is required to enter, though Ontario Provincial Park annual passes can be obtained online or onsite if staff are present at the gate. The park is a great place for migrants, especially warblers and sparrows. Tour the campgrounds, focusing on the sheltered edges of forest and shrub and any feeders that campers have up, and take advantage of as many of the trails as you have time for.

Just outside of Wheatley, check the field on the south side of Hwy. 3, just east of where Campers Cove Rd. intersects, for breeding Dickcissels. This is the province's most reliable spot for the species. The regenerating field can be good for other grassland species, such as Grasshopper and Field Sparrows and American Woodcock. This area can also be superb in the fall for migrating raptors. Days following a cold front with northwest winds are best.

GETTING THERE

To get to the area, exit Hwy. 401 in Tilbury (exits 56 and 63) and take County Road (CR) 1/Wheatley Rd. south to the town of Wheatley. Hillman Marsh is located southwest of town and can be accessed by staying on CR 1, then turning west (right) onto Deer Run Rd. before turning left again (south) onto Mersea Rd. 19.

WHEATLEY

HILLMAN MARSH

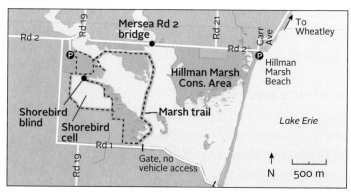

5
LAKE ST. CLAIR

OVERVIEW

With some of the most intact and biologically diverse wetlands in the province (and in Canada, for that matter), Lake St. Clair is a must for all birders. Although what was historically marsh and expansive prairie has now largely been converted to intensive agriculture, the remaining marshes are protected, primarily through private hunt clubs and the St. Clair National Wildlife Area (NWA) operated by the Canadian Wildlife Service.

The region provides the only location in southern Ontario for breeding Yellow-headed Blackbirds and is a major nesting stronghold for several rare marsh birds, including King Rail, Least Bittern, and Forster's Tern. The area is also recognized as the Eastern Lake St. Clair Important Bird and Biodiversity Area (IBA), in large part because of its importance for breeding marsh species and migratory waterfowl. Globally significant numbers of waterfowl are present in spring and fall, with counts of more than 30,000 Canvasbacks and 10,000 Tundra Swans. The region is also host to continentally significant numbers of migrant shorebirds in the spring, with up to 3.5% of the North American Black-bellied Plover population passing through in late May.

In early spring, tens of thousands of ducks and geese start to arrive as soon as Lake St. Clair opens up. April and early May bring back typical marsh-breeding birds, including an abundance of Common Yellowthroats, Marsh Wrens, and Swamp Sparrows that serenade visitors at pretty much every wetland. Stands of forest can also be excellent places for migrant songbirds because the region is so deforested that remaining tracts of forest are islands of refuge for migrant forest birds passing through. Fall is a protracted affair, as the surrounding lakes moderate the climate significantly and the region is one of the warmest in the province. Songbirds start passing through in earnest by late August, peaking from mid-September to mid-October. At this time of year, you'll see the first movement of waterfowl, and the numbers of ducks and geese really build through the late fall into early December, before freeze-up.

Winter is generally short and relatively mild. The large agricultural fields can have good numbers of Snowy Owls in irruptions as well as an abundance of wintering sparrows, such as American Tree Sparrows and Dark-eyed Juncos, in shrubland. Snow Buntings, Horned Larks, and Lapland Longspurs can also be found in the area, though they are more hit or miss.

The marshes around Lake St. Clair are one of the best spots in the province to
see the Common Gallinule, once known as the Common Moorhen.

Summer in this area is hot and long and provides a great opportunity to hone your marsh-birding skills. Forster's and Black Terns are common in the large wetlands, while Sora, Common Gallinule, Sandhill Crane, and both species of bitterns are regular in the region. The large wetlands have a few pairs of King Rails, but they are hard to find and shouldn't be expected.

BIRDING STRATEGY

The region is relatively large and will take a good part of a day to cover. While driving through the area, particularly in May, keep an eye out for shorebirds in the seasonally flooded fields (and upland shorebirds in drier sections). Waterfowl will frequent these same locations over a broader period, generally from when spring melt occurs until late April, and again from late September to freeze-up.

Start at the Tilbury Sewage Lagoons just north of the town of Tilbury on Clouthier St./Lakeshore Rd. 303, and drive around them (the roads are fine for virtually any car). Lately, water levels at the lagoons have been high; however, shorebirds do touch down here if the lagoons are on the drier side. All the regular "peeps" and plovers, as well as both yellowlegs, can be expected in May and throughout August and September. Purple Martins and Barn Swallows breed nearby and are common in the warmer months. The lagoons generally have a decent selection of ducks, most notably a Ruddy Duck (or two), some Wood Ducks, Double-crested Cormorants, and the odd Great Egret. In early fall, the lagoons have had both Snowy and Cattle Egrets in recent years and it is often possible to get good looks at the birds here.

Continuing from the sewage lagoons, we usually check Lighthouse Cove, only a few kilometres to the north where the Thames River empties into Lake St. Clair. From the lagoons, head west on Lakeshore Rd. 303 for 900 m/yds. Turn right onto Big Creek Rd. for 1.4 km (0.9 mi.), then turn left onto Essex County Road (CR) 2. Take this for 900 m/yds, before turning right onto CR 39 (the first road). Pay attention crossing the bridge shortly ahead, as egrets and cormorants are usually present in the spring and summer. Continue on CR 39 for 3.5 km (2.2 mi.) through the small town of Lighthouse Cove and follow the road to the dead end overlooking the mouth of the Thames River. The parking lot here provides a great vantage point for scoping the lake. In winter, when the river is open, this site hosts excellent numbers of gulls, in particular Glaucous Gulls, and sometimes as many as 10 or 20 Bald Eagles. In the summer Forster's Terns are common, while in migration you'll see decent numbers of Bonaparte's Gulls. There are usually a few Great Egrets along the river's edge too. Both Cattle Egret and Little Blue Heron have been found here recently, so be sure to scan the shoreline. Swallows also congregate in spring and fall, particularly during periods of cool, inclement weather.

Once you've had your fill of Lighthouse Cove, follow CR 39 south to CR 2. Take CR 2 left (east), towards Chatham for 12.5 km (7.8 mi.) (the road will change to CR 36). In Prairie Siding, turn left (north) onto Jacob Rd., which crosses the Thames River. As you're driving along CR 2 and 36, keep an eye out for egrets and herons along the river—we saw our first Snowy Egret following the river here. Take Jacob Rd. north for 2.1 km (1.3 mi.) before turning west (left) onto Pain Court Line.

Take Pain Court for 3.2 km (2 mi.), turn right onto Town Line Rd, and follow it for 3.1 km (1.9 mi.). Accessing the St. Clair NWA can be somewhat tricky—there is a small laneway/bridge across the canal, which is Balmoral Line. Once across the canal, make an immediate right to follow the canal north to the parking lot. From there a trail through the wildlife area leads to an observation tower. A walk here at dawn or dusk during the breeding season is almost guaranteed to net you both species of bitterns, Soras, Virginia Rails, Sandhill Cranes, and Common Gallinules, while you might encounter a King Rail if you are lucky. Back at the parking lot, keep an eye on the willows that line the road along the canal, as they can be surprisingly active with songbirds in migration. Note that ticks can be abundant here, so take necessary precautions.

Leaving St. Clair NWA, continue north on Town Line Rd. for 2.5 km (1.6 mi.), where the road will turn 90 degrees to the east and become Rivard Line. As you drive, watch for herons and egrets in the canal to your left. In summer, the area at the corner of Town Line Rd. and Rivard Line can sometimes have Yellow-billed Cuckoos. Continuing on, take Rivard Line east for 7.5 km (4.7 mi.), where you'll reach a stop sign at Winter Line (CR 34). Turn left (north) onto Winter Line, and take this for 5.5 km (3.4 mi.) to Angler Line. Turn left (west) onto Angler Line and drive towards the dead end at the lake. As you drive down Angler Line, again keep an eye on the canal to your left (south) for herons and egrets and anything else that might be trying to hide along the water's edge. The trailhead for the Waterfront Trail will appear after 1.8 km (1.1 mi.) on Angler Line and is a nice leisurely walk of 1.3 km (0.8 mi.) north to the town of Mitchell's Bay. The trail follows a wooded canal and then opens up with a view of the lake as you approach Mitchell's Bay. The open areas are excellent places to scan the lake for terns, egrets, and herons, while the canal, particularly in migration, can be excellent for passerines. Be sure to look over to the agricultural fields on your right, as they can sometimes have Yellow-headed Blackbirds.

Back at Angler Line, continue driving towards the lake. Not far from the trailhead, the marsh opens up on the north side of the road and provides a great opportunity to look for marsh birds such as Pied-billed Grebes, Green Herons, and the ever incessant Marsh Wrens and Common Yellowthroats. Where the road dead-ends is a vantage point from which to view the lake. Be sure to bring your scope, as the offshore islands have nesting Yellow-headed Blackbirds and you'll likely see feeding Forster's Terns and a few Black-crowned Night-Herons. Common Gallinules are also regular here but tend to stay closer to shore. If you drive across the canal to the south and continue 200 m/yds to the very end, you will sometimes find Yellow-headed Blackbirds feeding on people's lawns.

Heading out from Angler Line, continue back to Winter Line. Take Winter Line one concession north to Bay Line, and then follow Bay Line west to the small town of Mitchell's Bay. Where Bay Line dead-ends at Lake St. Clair is a small park where the town wharf provides great views of the lake. Thousands of ducks are generally offshore here in early spring and late fall—particularly Canvasbacks and Redheads. Bald Eagles nest nearby and can be seen at any time of the year. Access the Waterfront Trail off Park St., directly off Bay Line.

GETTING THERE

From either direction, take Hwy. 401 west, following signs for Windsor, and get off the highway at exit 56 for Tilbury (CR 42).

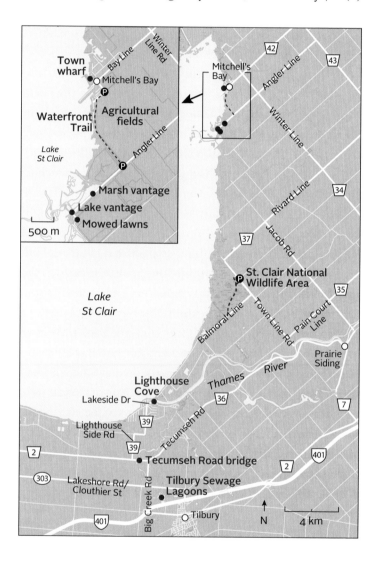

6

RONDEAU PROVINCIAL PARK

OVERVIEW

Without a doubt, Rondeau Provincial Park should be near the top of every birder's list of places to visit in Ontario. Traditionally, most birders passed by Rondeau, but increasingly it is not only a stop on a birding trip, but the destination. And for good reason: the number of waterfowl here can be staggering, as can the number and diversity of migrant songbirds. The park is on par with nearby Point Pelee National Park (Chapter 3) and Long Point (Chapter 11) as a migration hotspot, and a good day in May or September can leave you asking, "Pelee who?" It is also the best-known and most accessible place in the country to see Prothonotary Warblers. As an added bonus, the list of breeding species is one of the best in the province.

Each time you visit it still feels like you've stumbled upon a secret birding spot—although word is starting to get out.

Known by the French who settled this area as the "Bay of Pines," Rondeau literally means "round water," which describes the shape of the harbour sheltered by the peninsula. The area's European history dates back to the 1700s, the British navy harvesting the area's large White Pines to make ship masts during the War of 1812, and other exploits. Today the park is a popular location for cottagers and campers, primarily in the summer months. From a natural heritage perspective, the park is located in the heart of the Carolinian Zone and moderated by the warm waters of Lake Erie. Here you'll see some of the best examples of rich deciduous Carolinian forests with towering Tulip Trees. The park and its adjacent locations provide a "full-service" birding experience, meaning that in every season you can expect some of the best birding in the province.

The breeding season draws an excellent mix of forest and marsh birds. Throughout the forested areas, the park is home to many rare southern species: Acadian Flycatcher, White-eyed Vireo, Tufted Titmouse, and Hooded and Prothonotary Warblers are present annually. The more common Eastern Wood-Pewee, Wood Thrush, Blue-gray Gnatcatcher, and Scarlet Tanager also visit the park at this time of year. At the marsh around Rondeau Bay, you are likely to see breeding Black Terns, Least and American Bitterns, and, if you're lucky, King Rails.

The park is a major hotspot for birds that are either crossing Lake Erie or funnelling along the north shore in spring and fall, and migration is an excellent time to bird here.

Prothonotary Warblers got Ken hooked on birding, and Rondeau is perhaps the best site in the province to see them. Look for these birds particularly on the Tulip Tree Trail. KENNETH BURRELL

Typically, late April through mid-May and September are the best times to visit for the highest numbers and diversity; however, any time from early April to late May and from late August to early November can be excellent.

Shorebirding in May and in late July to October is underrated here, but the shoreline and Blenheim Sewage Lagoons offer excellent birding and shouldn't be overlooked. You can also watch for hawks, though most observers travel to either Hawk Cliff (Chapter 10) or Holiday Beach (Chapter 1).

Winter is a slower time of year here, as at many locations along the north shore of Lake Erie. Residents, such as Pileated and Red-bellied Woodpeckers, Tufted Titmice, and Carolina Wrens, are present, as are lingering over-winterers like Yellow-rumped Warblers and Ruby-crowned Kinglets, albeit in lower numbers.

BIRDING STRATEGY

From the Rondeau Provincial Park gate, start at the pull-in parking spot directly to the south. This location provides a view of Rondeau Bay and can be a good place to scan for waterfowl and gulls. The bay can be teeming with thousands of Tundra Swans and ducks: Greater Scaup, American Wigeon, Canvasback, and Redhead are some of the more common species to be expected from March to mid-April and again from mid-October to freeze-up (generally mid-December). Take your time scanning the bay: Eurasian Wigeon is found here annually, mixed in with the big duck flocks.

South of the park gate, stop at the intersection of Rondeau Ave. and Rondeau Rd., where the park store is located. The parking lot here provides another great vantage of Rondeau

Bay, which should be scoped for waterfowl and other water-birds. Heading east on Rondeau Ave., the Maintenance Loop will be on your right (south) and can be accessed by taking the first driveway south. A short trail here can be excellent in migration for warblers and sparrows. In particular, watch for Red-headed Woodpeckers in spring migration and during the breeding season.

Directly to the east of the Maintenance Loop is a drive of 500 m/yds that extends to the Pony Barns. While there aren't any ponies, in spring and fall migration this spot can be absolutely fantastic, especially during days of strong wind (it is quite sheltered). All of the rare southern species, like Worm-eating, Kentucky, and Yellow-throated Warblers, have been seen here, and the songbirding in general is excellent, with over 20 species of warbler and all the regular *Catharus* thrushes to be expected in peak songbird migration.

Leaving the Pony Barns, head west on Rondeau Ave. and turn left (south) on Rondeau Rd. Take your first right to cut over to Water St. and then turn left. After a short distance, you'll see a picnic area in an open area on the west side of the road and the entrance to the Marsh Trail. This trail provides an excellent opportunity to see virtually every southern Ontario wetland species, including King Rails. Be warned, however, that the trail is long (7.5 km/4.7 mi. one way) and dead-ends.

Continue south on Rondeau Rd. for 1.5 km (0.9 mi.) to the intersection with Bennet Rd. The entrance to the Spicebush Trail is on your right (west). This trail is another migration hotspot, as it follows one of the park's many sloughs and is generally excellent for songbirding. The western edge of the trail is located in more marshy habitat and can provide a good view of the sky. Eastern Wood-Pewees, Great Crested Flycatchers, and White-breasted Nuthatches breed here, and keeping an eye overhead can sometimes yield glimpses of the odd Northern Harrier or Sharp-shinned Hawk.

Back at the trail entrance, walk across Rondeau Rd. and head straight (east) along Bennet Rd. This road is closed in May when Prothonotary Warblers and Acadian Flycatchers are nesting, but otherwise it is another good place to bird in any season. In the winter, you'll see typical woodland species, such as Pileated Woodpecker, Tufted Titmouse, White-breasted Nuthatch, and Hairy Woodpecker. In spring, the road offers leisurely birding, with many of the same species as at other migration hotspots within Rondeau.

Continue on Rondeau Rd. south for 2.2 km (1.4 mi.), where it turns 90 degrees east and becomes Gardiner Ave. At this junction is a parking lot for the South Point Trail, a U-shaped route that loops back to the southern end of Lakeshore Rd. (see below). However, follow Gardiner Ave. for a few hundred metres to arrive at the Visitor Centre (vc). Here you'll find year-round feeders. In winter, the feeders can be packed with lingering sparrows and blackbirds, including Eastern Towhee, Chipping Sparrow, and Rusty and Red-winged Blackbirds. The feeders can be equally awesome in spring, with point-blank views of Indigo Bunting and Rose-breasted Grosbeak. Across Gardiner Ave. from the vc is a large open space where migrant songbirds often congregate in large numbers, particularly in September and early October.

After you've had your fill of the vc, walk the Tulip Tree Trail, an easy 1.2 km (0.8 mi.) loop. The trail meanders through several wet sloughs and can be excellent for migrant songbirds, including vireos, thrushes, warblers, and flycatchers. In April, you'll find the odd Louisiana Waterthrush in the sloughs, but be warned that Northerns will start showing up by late April and it can be difficult to tell these species apart during the two weeks or so that they overlap. The trail also provides some of the most reliable and easy-to-access locations in the province for breeding Prothonotary Warblers, as 1–2 pairs generally nest in the boxes specially put up for them along the trail.

Leaving Tulip Tree Trail and the vc, take Lakeshore Rd. south to where it dead-ends. En route are several beach-access points that provide good vantages of the lake and can be productive in any season for a mix of waterbirds, including Horned Grebe, the odd scoter, and good numbers of both Common and Red-breasted Mergansers. At the end of Lakeshore Rd. is the other trailhead for South Point Trail (noted earlier). Walking south along the trail is especially recommended in migration, as the shrubby areas are particularly favoured by migrants and vagrant passerines. White-eyed Vireos and Yellow-breasted Chats both show up here quite regularly as well and nest sporadically. We typically only walk to the first side-trail that heads to the lake (~1.5 km/0.9 mi.); however, the entire 8 km (5 mi.) loop can be excellent and extends past the southernmost part of the park, opposite Erieau.

Back at Lakeshore Rd. continue north, past the vc. The campground at the north end of the park is the last place we generally check and it's a good spot for sparrows in migration and in winter. Red-headed Woodpeckers can also be seen fairly reliably in spring and summer.

After leaving the park, we typically check Bate's Marsh, which is the causeway just north of the park along Kent Bridge Rd. Local conservation groups have done their best to eradicate Common Reed, and Great Blue Herons, American Coots, and Belted Kingfishers along with numerous Marsh Wrens, Common Yellowthroats, and Swamp Sparrows are present here.

Continue on Kent Bridge Rd. to the second road—New Scotland Line. Take this west (left) to Shrewsbury, where you can access the town dock by turning east (left) on Brock St. towards Rondeau Bay. This spot provides a great vantage point to scan the tens of thousands of ducks (and often thousands of Tundra Swans) here in early spring and late fall. Eurasian Wigeons visit annually, though picking one out from among 10,000+ ducks can be challenging and a scope is highly recommended!

Leaving Shrewsbury, you'll have to zig-zag along New Scotland Line, Fargo Rd., Bisnett Line, and Erieau Rd. to get to the town of Erieau. Just before you enter Erieau, you'll notice a marsh on your right (south)—this is McGeachy Pond. There's a small trail along the lake side of the marsh here that can be productive in migration and for lingering songbirds in early winter. The pond itself is generally good for dabblers, Redheads, and several pairs of Mute Swans. Just past McGeachy Pond and on the opposite side of the road is the Erieau Marsh Trail, a walking trail that can be productive for Sora, Virginia Rail, both Least and American Bitterns, and a pair of annual nesting Great Horned Owls.

Continuing along Erieau Rd., the townsite of Erieau is opposite the terminus of Rondeau Provincial Park. Here are several excellent locations that can be good at any time of the year, primarily for waterbirds. The channel separating Erieau from Rondeau Provincial Park is a must to check. Countless rarities have been seen here, and it is a particularly great location for rare gulls and terns, with Little Gulls and the odd Laughing Gull showing up. Checking the beach at the channel can also be good for shorebirds in late spring and autumn, while the bay provides opportunities to see thousands of ducks, similar to other locations around Rondeau Bay.

Capping off the Rondeau experience are the Blenheim Sewage Lagoons, located on the southwest side of Blenheim, along Lagoon Rd. a kilometre west of Hwy. 3. To enter the lagoons you must register with the town to obtain a permit and lock combination—the office is located at 35 Talbot St. W, but we'd recommend getting your paperwork in order before the trip. The lagoons themselves provide one of the best locations in southwestern Ontario for shorebirds, being the most reliable spot for Wilson's Phalarope along with other less common shorebirds such as Long-billed Dowitcher and White-rumped and Baird's Sandpipers, and rarities like Willet, American Avocet, and Buff-breasted Sandpiper. While excellent for shorebirds, the lagoons have also had their share of exciting herons, ducks, and grebes and are worth checking anytime outside of winter.

GETTING THERE

Rondeau Provincial Park is best accessed via Hwy. 401 and is a 1.5-hour drive from London and Windsor. Access is easiest by taking Kent Bridge Rd. (exit 101) from Hwy. 401 and travelling south for 15 minutes.

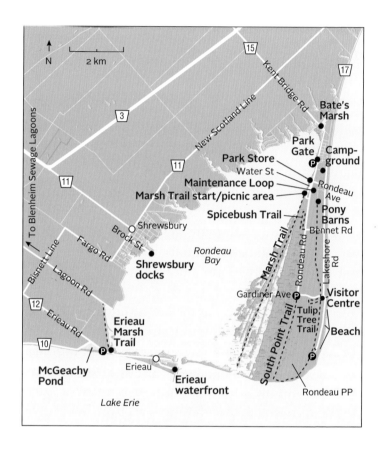

7
SARNIA AND AREA

OVERVIEW

Located where Lake Huron flows into the St. Clair River, Sarnia is ideally situated for birding in all seasons and is one of our "hidden" favourites. In migration, large concentrations of waterbirds occur along Point Edward and the lakeshore, while the fall pelagic birding rivals the likes of Hamilton—though don't tell the birders in Hamilton that. Songbird migration is equally impressive, with lakeshore woodlots being particularly active, and spring hawk flights occur along the lakeshore too, especially during strong southwesterly winds. In winter there is excellent birding along the river and the lakeshore. And during the breeding season, the numerous woodlots in the area can be good places to spot rare southern breeders.

Visitors to this area are often struck by the scale of industry in Sarnia, a city better known for its major petrochemical companies than for its birding. The best birding areas are located largely on the periphery of the city and along the waterfront.

BIRDING STRATEGY

Depending on where you're arriving from, your starting point on this roughly counter-clockwise route will vary. We usually begin at the parking lot for Perch Creek Habitat Management Area, on Churchill Line just 400 m/yds east of Blackwell Sideroad.

A series of trails runs through the habitat management area, providing summer birders with an assortment of old-field/shrub species, such as Field Sparrows, Eastern Towhees, and Indigo Buntings. Listen for the ping-pong-like song of Field Sparrows in more open areas; in the wooded sections, keep an ear out for the plaintive *pee-weee* of the Eastern Wood-Pewee. In winter, the conifers throughout can be home to several owl species, with Northern Saw-whet and Long-eared being the most regular. They can be particularly challenging to find, and checking each conifer individually is the best (though time-consuming) strategy. To avoid harassing them unnecessarily, remember to keep your distance and turn off the flash on your camera.

Driving north along Blackwell Sideroad (west of Perch Creek), you'll quickly find yourself beside a large solar farm, on your left, while the old Sarnia landfill will be on your right. In late fall and winter, watch for Snowy and Short-eared Owls over these fields: both are present most winters. Dusk is generally the best time to look for the Short-eareds, whereas Northern Harriers and the odd Rough-legged Hawk and

Wintering ducks, like Redheads (background) and Canvasbacks (foreground), are abundant along the St. Clair River. JOSHUA D. VANDERMEULEN

Northern Shrike are around in the daytime in winter. In summer, Bobolink and Eastern Meadowlark are common here, along with Grasshopper Sparrow and—in irruption years—a pair (or two) of Dickcissels.

Continue farther north along Blackwell Sideroad, passing over Hwy. 402, and watch for a small laneway on your left signed for the Wawanosh Wetlands Conservation Area (650 m/yds past Hwy. 402). A hidden gem, the wetlands have recorded close to 250 species! A series of walking trails with a total distance of 2.5 km (1.6 mi.) loop around the constructed wetlands, which provide a great spot to see marsh and old-field species. Wood Ducks breed here, and in migration, Ruddy Ducks and Buffleheads are regular. The complex is one of the best local sites for marsh-breeding species, with Sora, Virginia Rail, and Least Bittern all present. Shrubland and old-field species also breed in numbers in these wetlands, including Willow Flycatcher, Orchard and Baltimore Orioles, and Swamp Sparrow, while in spring and fall the conservation area can be an excellent spot to see migrants too.

From the Wawanosh Wetlands, continue north on Blackwell Sideroad for 2.9 km (1.8 mi.), where you'll turn left (west) onto Lakeshore Rd./Lambton County Road (CR) 7. Take this road west for 6.5 km (4 mi.). As Lakeshore Rd. curves south, turn right almost immediately onto Charlesworth Lane, which will lead you to Canatara Park. With over 34 species of warblers among the 250+ species seen over the years, Canatara Park is the premier spot in the Sarnia area for migrants. Generally speaking, the best time to bird here is from mid-April to late May and again from early September to late October.

Walking throughout the park, particularly around Lake Chipican, regularly reveals all the expected long-distance—or neotropic—migrants, such as warblers and flycatchers, and the short-distance—or temperate—migrants, such as sparrows. In May, the park can rival major hotspots like Point Pelee (Chapter 3) and Long Point (Chapter 11), with warblers, grosbeaks, buntings, vireos, and flycatchers all well represented. The park's location adjacent to Lake Huron also makes it a refuge for migrant passerines travelling along the lakeshore in spring and fall, a fact that makes this spot the go-to for local birders interested in these species. Sparrows in particular can be abundant here in October.

Located only a few short minutes from Canatara Park is Point Edward, one of the best spots on the Great Lakes from which to watch waterbirds on the lake. It rivals the likes of Van Wagner's Beach in Hamilton (Chapter 14). From the west side of Canatara, head south on Sandy Lane, which fairly quickly becomes Alfred St. Take this road to Victoria Ave. and turn right to travel west for 600 m/yds, before turning right onto Fort St. Follow Fort St. all the way to the lake and you'll come to a parking lot. Scanning the lake from here in fall (late August to early November), particularly on days with strong north or northwest winds, is ideal for spotting pelagics. All three jaegers, Sabine's Gulls, and Black-legged Kittiwakes are regularly seen here in the fall. The number of ducks can also be impressive, with thousands of Long-tailed Ducks in late fall and in warmer winters too. All three scoters are usually present in late fall and early winter, along with the odd Red-necked Grebe. In summer, Peregrine Falcons nest to the south and are most frequently seen flying along the river and/or perching on the Bluewater Bridge, which spans the St. Clair River to Michigan.

Heading back along Victoria Ave., turn south onto St. Clair St. and follow it to Front St. Turning right (south) will bring you under Hwy. 402, and after a short distance Centennial Park will be on your right (west). The park surrounds Sarnia Bay and is a great spot for waterbirds. For the easiest access point, turn right onto Exmouth St., turn left onto Harbour Rd., and follow it to the parking lots at the end of Seaway Rd. In late fall and winter when the water is open, the area can be excellent for a variety of diving ducks, including Canvasbacks, Redheads, Greater Scaups, Long-tailed Ducks, and Red-breasted Mergansers. In the early winter lingering waterbirds, such as Pied-billed and Red-necked Grebes and Double-crested Cormorants, are often present. Gulls are also well represented, particularly around freeze-up, and good numbers of Glaucous, Iceland, and Lesser Black-backed are regularly seen. Franklin's Gulls and Black-legged Kittiwakes are also spotted occasionally, though much more rarely than these other species. In spring, the area has had decent numbers of Forster's Terns considering that the closest breeding colony is at Lake St. Clair (Chapter 5). Any stands of trees in spring and fall can also be good for migrant songbirds.

Continuing on from Centennial Park, take Front St. south to Christina St. Take a right onto Christina and follow it until Clifford St., where you turn left. At the stoplights, turn right (south) onto Vidal St. and follow it south; eventually it will turn into the St. Clair Pkwy. We recommend that you drive slowly along this stretch of the river, pulling off to the side of the road as frequently as you can to scan the river, as waterbird concentrations change constantly. In late winter the ice conditions will affect bird movement; taking this into consideration should help in locating waterbirds on the river. In particular, look for birds in the open stretches of river. Along the parkway, both Guthrie and Willow Parks provide good spots to stop and get out and scan leisurely. The river from Sarnia south all the way to Port Lambton is approximately 33 km (20.5 mi.), and it is worth checking the entire length if time permits. The river is known for its wintering ducks, especially Canvasbacks and Long-tailed Ducks. Scoters and the odd Horned or Red-necked Grebe are also usually around each winter, while Barrow's Goldeneyes, King Eiders, and Harlequin Ducks are possible, but quite rare. Gulls are the other draw in the winter, with good numbers of Glaucous, Iceland, and Lesser Black-backeds around. The number of rare gulls seen along the St. Clair River rivals Niagara, with both Ivory and Ross's Gulls seen here among the 15+ species of gulls.

GETTING THERE
Easily located, Sarnia is approximately 100 km (60 mi.) west of London. Access is easiest by taking Hwy. 402 west.

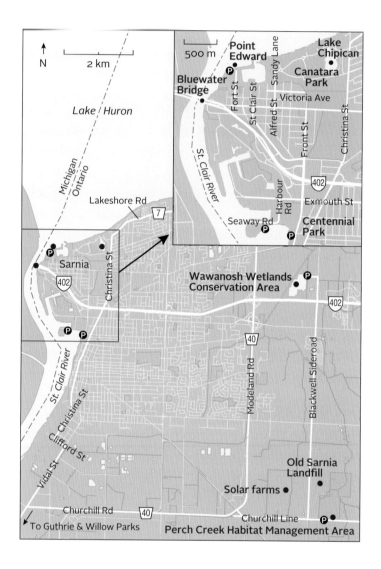

8

KETTLE POINT AND PINERY PROVINCIAL PARK

OVERVIEW

This section of the Lake Huron shoreline is a natural heritage gem, with extensive tracts of forest nestled between the Chippewas of Kettle and Stony Point First Nation and the town of Grand Bend. In between lie the town of Port Franks, a former provincial park (Ipperwash), and an existing provincial park (the Pinery). The region offers a glimpse into the importance of natural land conservancy, specifically along the Great Lakes, and provides a stark contrast to much of southern Ontario's intensive agriculture and urban sprawl.

Birding this area can yield exceptional fall waterbird counts, thousands of spring migrant Tundra Swans, rare Carolinian breeders, and excellent songbirding in both spring and fall. We first visited this area with our dad during a spring break when we were in public school, to help out with the Tundra Swan festival, which was run by Pinery Provincial Park. We got a good introduction to the area then, as thousands of Tundra Swans forage annually in the fields nearby, rivalling the likes of Long Point (Chapter 11) and Lake St. Clair (Chapter 5), and we've been coming back ever since.

Located only an hour from London, the area is easily accessible. In summer, Grand Bend and the Pinery especially are overrun with vacationers and campers, but the rest of the year sees few tourists except on long weekends. As a whole, the region receives less birding coverage than locations on Lakes Ontario and Erie, though it offers comparably excellent birding year-round.

BIRDING STRATEGY

Starting at the corner of Indian Line and West Ipperwash Rd., just northwest (200 m/yds) of Hwy. 21 and Lakeshore Rd./ County Road (CR) 7, continue west on Indian Line until you reach the lake (2.4 km/1.5 mi.). Follow Indian Line north and it becomes Lake Rd. As you travel along this road, keep an eye to the west for ducks and herons. Great Egrets are usually present in late summer and early fall, as are Caspian and Common Terns. After 4.5 km (2.8 mi.) you'll reach the very tip of Kettle Point, which is marked only by a 120-degree turn to your right (east). Park on the west side of the road by the large cement blocks and scan the lake from the shoreline. In

▶ Among the quintessential signs of spring in southwestern Ontario, particularly in the Kettle Point area, are large flocks of Tundra Swans in March and April.
MICHAEL BURRELL

The Prairie Warbler is a rare breeder at Pinery Provincial Park; listen for its rising *zee-zee-zee-zee* song along the shoreline where Red Cedars are found.
MICHAEL BURRELL

fall, you'll likely see an absurd number of waterbirds. Days of strong northwest winds following cold fronts can produce pelagic birds: all three jaegers, Sabine's Gulls, and Black-legged Kittiwakes are routinely found here from late August through early November, though spotting them requires patience. Lake watching here rivals the likes of Van Wagner's Beach in Hamilton (Chapter 14) and Point Edward in Sarnia (Chapter 7) but is far less well known.

Driving slowly throughout the interior in June can be a

good way to find rare Carolinian breeders, so keep an ear out for the buzzy *zee zee zee ziziziZI* song of the Cerulean Warbler and the whistled *ta-whit ta-whit ta-whit-tee-yo* of the Hooded Warbler. Both are typically present alongside more common forest birds, including Eastern Wood-Pewee, Wood Thrush, Ovenbird, and Yellow-throated Vireo.

Follow the shoreline east from here, along Lake Rd., London Rd., West Ipperwash Rd., West Parkway Dr., and East Parkway Dr. Each of these roads requires small jogs to stay along the shoreline, but these are clearly visible from the preceding stop sign. Once on E. Parkway Dr., take the second road on your right (south)—Richardson Dr.—and follow it to the very end. Park in the small lot for the Nature Conservancy of Canada's Ipperwash Dunes and Swales property and its trails. Following the trails to the east, where the campground of the former Ipperwash Provincial Park was, look for migrant songbirds in spring and fall. The wooded sections to the south provide good habitat for northern breeders, such as Canada and Black-and-white Warblers. Hooded Warblers are also present in low numbers here.

Heading back to E. Parkway Dr., continue east along the lake: several lake-access points can be good places to scan for ducks and loons in migration. The road will turn south and become Army Camp Rd./CR 3, which you follow to Lakeshore Rd. Turn left and travel east 3.2 km (2 mi.) to Outer Dr., where you turn left (north). The Lambton County Heritage Forest and other adjoining conservation lands will quickly be on your right (east). Park at any of the trailheads along Outer Dr. that are signed from the road.

Walking the trails through the forest should net more

Hooded Warblers, as well as Acadian Flycatchers—several pairs typically nest here, so pay close attention to wooded streams with stands of Eastern Hemlock, as these are prime spots for them. Listen for their loud *peetSup* calls. Cerulean Warblers can also be present, though they are harder to find. Keep a careful ear out for Tufted Titmice too, as their *Pee-ter-pee-ter-pee-ter* song can "blend" into the background of the forest, while Scarlet Tanagers, Wood Thrushes, and Great Crested Flycatchers are relatively common.

Continuing north on Outer Dr., you'll pass over a bridge and skirt "L" Lake. A good assortment of wetland bird species, including Sandhill Crane and Wood Duck, nest here. In migration the pond should have a number of ducks, including Ring-necked Duck, Bufflehead, and American Wigeon. As you continue east along Outer Dr., the road becomes Riverside Dr. when you enter Port Franks. The beach at the river mouth can be good for gulls in migration and winter and is always worth checking. From the main intersection in Port Franks, go south on Superior St., which becomes Port Franks Rd. The Port Franks Community Centre on your right (west) is a good place to park to access one of the trails for the Lambton County Heritage Forest and adjoining properties, though there are several other trailheads off Port Franks Rd. farther south. These trails link up with the ones you accessed from Outer Dr. and will net many of the same species.

Once back on Hwy. 21/Lakeshore Rd., continue east (left), taking the highway for 8.5 km (5.3 mi.) to the entrance into Pinery Provincial Park. There's a small entrance fee for the park, payable at the park gate. Within the park are 10 hiking trails spanning more than 15 km (9 mi.). The Riverside and Carolinian Trails are our favourites and have many of southern Ontario's typical woodland breeding birds: Wood Thrush, Scarlet Tanager, Ovenbird, and Eastern Wood-Pewee. In the more open habitats, species like Field Sparrow, Eastern Towhee, and Indigo Bunting can be common, along with the odd Red-headed Woodpecker. Tufted Titmouse is common throughout the park, but the best place to see it is at the Visitor Centre, which has several year-round feeders. Yellow-throated Vireos are also present along the Old Ausable Channel. During the breeding season, the park has a very healthy population of Eastern Whip-poor-wills, whose loud song is hard to miss if you stay until dark.

One of the things that the Pinery is known for is its beach; thousands of beach-goers come here in the summer (typically July and August), so keep this in mind. During spring and fall, however, the lake produces your typical waterbirds (e.g., Common Loons, Horned Grebes, and Bonaparte's Gulls), while shorebirds can also be present. In recent years a few pairs of Prairie Warblers have nested along the sensitive dune habitat, with the Dunes Beach parking lot your best bet to find this rare species.

Heading out of the Pinery, continue east along Hwy. 21/ Lakeshore Rd. for a kilometre to Greenway Rd./CR 5. Turn right (east), and you'll be smack dab in the middle of the historical Lake Smith—a formerly extensive bog that's now been drained for agriculture. This area hosts thousands of Tundra Swans annually, with the best time to spot them being from early March to mid-April. Among the swans will be a myriad of puddle ducks, with excellent numbers of Northern Pintail, American Wigeon, and Green-winged Teal, among others.

If there are any flooded sections of the fields, make sure to scan these spots, as shorebirds can also be present any time after late March, when the first Pectoral Sandpipers and both yellowlegs start to arrive. The best areas along Greenway Rd. are typically 1–2 km (0.6–1.2 mi.) and 4 km (2.4 mi.) from Hwy. 21. However, any of the fields in this area can be good for waterfowl and are usually worth driving in spring.

After moving on from the "good" area of Greenway Rd., continue east to Mollard Line. At Mollard Line, turn north (left). The Grand Bend Sewage Lagoons will be on your left (west) after 5.5 km (3.4 mi.). A small parking lot is readily visible; park here and walk around the lagoons. These can be a good place for waterfowl (early spring and late fall) and shorebirds (late spring and early fall), with an excellent assortment of rarities having been spotted over the years. Sparrows in particular favour the shrubby habitat along the edge of the lagoons, while Eastern Kingbirds gather along the fence lines in early August.

GETTING THERE

The region is about an hour from London and 1.5 hours from Kitchener-Waterloo. From Hwy. 402, exit at Hwy. 21 and go north on this highway through the town of Forest. Turn left off Hwy. 21 at Lakeshore Rd./CR 7, and almost immediately go north (right) onto West Ipperwash Rd.

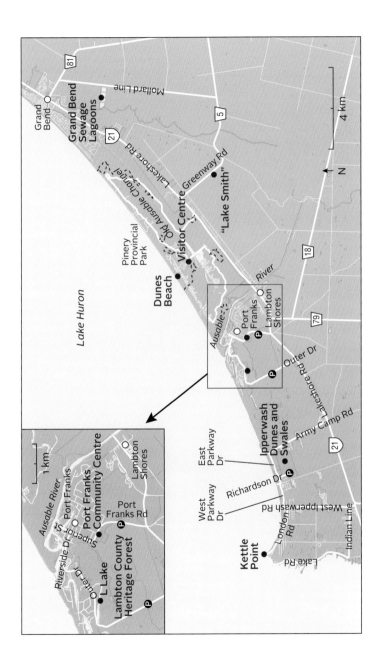

Grand Bend

81

Grand Bend Sewage Lagoons

Mollard Line

21

Lakeshore Rd

5

Old Ausable Channel

Greenway Rd

Visitor Centre

"Lake Smith"

Pinery Provincial Park

Lake Huron

Dunes Beach

River

18

Ausable

Port Franks

Lambton Shores

79

Outer Dr

Army Camp Rd

Ipperwash Dunes and Swales

21

East Parkway Dr

Richardson Dr

West Parkway Dr

West Ipperwash Rd

Kettle Point

London Rd

Lake Rd

Indian Line

N

4 km

1 km

Ausable River

Port Franks

Lambton Shores

Port Franks Community Centre

Port Franks Rd

Superior St

Riverside Dr

Outer Dr

L Lake

Lambton County Heritage Forest

9

SOUTHERN BRUCE COUNTY

OVERVIEW

Originally part of an area known as the Queen's Bush, what we now refer to as Bruce County was formed geopolitically in the mid-1800s. John Riley perhaps best describes this area— referring to it as Huronia in his book *The Once and Future Great Lakes Country: An Ecological History*—as picturesque rolling fields and forest, reminiscent of Europe from the 1600s. The spread of European diseases that had wiped out much of the Indigenous population by the mid-1700s coincided with the arrival of the first European settlers who came to farm. Today, the area is largely agricultural, with a substantial but

◄ Upland Sandpipers like to survey their breeding territories from the tops of perches, like fence posts, so watch for them whenever driving through grassland habitat like along the J/I Line. BRANDON HOLDEN

decreasing number of cattle farms, many of which are being converted to more lucrative cash crops. The area is also a popular summer destination for cottagers and beach-goers and a year-round hotspot for birders. Over 330 species have been found here, yet far fewer birders visit the county than other areas in southern Ontario.

Bruce County is a fabulous area stretching close to 150 km (93 mi.) from south to north, with rich farmland and scattered forests in the south and the highly forested Niagara Escarpment in the north. We've focused on southern Bruce County, covering an area roughly from Kincardine in the south to Sauble Beach in the north, because it is more accessible and offers more varied birding opportunities year-round than the northern part of the county. The area is best explored in the breeding season as well as during spring and fall migrations, when it is particularly excellent for a variety of grassland and second-growth species like Chestnut-sided and Golden-winged Warblers, American Redstarts, Wilson's Snipes, Upland Sandpipers, Grasshopper and Clay-colored Sparrows, Eastern Meadowlarks, and Bobolinks. In winter, the agricultural fields can be productive for winter raptors like Rough-legged Hawks and Snowy Owls, while the Bruce Nuclear Generating Station keeps the surrounding bay (Baie du Doré) free of ice, attracting lots of eagles, waterfowl, and gulls.

BIRDING STRATEGY

Starting in Kincardine, you'll want to check the sewage lagoons and the town harbour. The lagoons, located off Bruce Ave. in Legion Park, have had over 225 species alone! To access them, park at the baseball diamond and then follow the trail through the wooded area to the south. The lagoons' water levels are generally pretty high, and as a result we've never had good shorebirding here, though it is regularly excellent for waterbirds, with Greater White-fronted and Ross's Geese showing up on occasion as well as Eared Grebe. Trails alongside the lagoons allow you to get close to the cells through the adjacent forest, which can be good in migration for songbirds too.

Kincardine Harbour can be easily accessed from the lagoons by going west on Bruce Ave. and turning right (north) onto Penetangore Row, which becomes Huron Terrace. The best access is located along Station Beach Rd., off Huron Terrace. From the parking lot surrounding the marina, check the beach for shorebirds and gulls, while scoping the lake offshore for loons (Red-throated and Common) and grebes. A number of rarities have been seen here over the years, including Franklin's Gulls and Black-legged Kittiwakes.

From Kincardine, head north on County Road (CR) 23. After several kilometres you'll turn left (west) on CR 15, which takes you into Inverhuron. In town, follow Albert Rd., then Alma St. and Jordan Rd., to Inverhuron Provincial Park, a relatively small park that offers good camping and beach-going in the summer and is an excellent stopover site for songbirds in spring and fall. Despite its lack of birding coverage, the park has had two Kirtland's Warblers, which isn't as surprising as it seems when you consider that it's about as close as you can get in Ontario to their main breeding grounds in Michigan.

From Inverhuron, go north along Concession 2 and then Tie Rd. to Baie du Doré, which is only about five minutes ahead on the north side of the Bruce Generating Station. From the end of Baie du Doré Rd./Bruce Rd. 33, follow the bumpy road for 300 m/yds to the lake—be careful driving in, particularly after heavy snowfalls. In winter this is one of the best spots in the county to see waterbirds, as the warm-water outflow from the generating station keeps the bay free of ice and attracts large numbers of birds, particularly in cold winters. Over 20 Bald Eagles are regularly seen at this time of year, while the odd Little Gull shows up in addition to good counts of Glaucous Gulls. Waterfowl are also attracted here, with all three species of scoters, Common Goldeneyes, and the regular dabbling ducks too. In summer, American Bitterns can be heard in the marsh booming away, while Common Terns forage not far offshore or perch on the scattered rocks in the bay.

From Baie du Doré, head east on Bruce Rd. 33 and Concession 6 until you reach the J/I Line. To birders from the area, the J/I Line is synonymous with some of the best grassland birding in Ontario, rivalling the Carden Alvar (Chapter 18) and the Napanee Plain (Chapter 22). Travelling north up the J/I Line between mid-May and early July should yield all the typical Ontario grassland species, including Upland Sandpiper, Brewer's Blackbird, Grasshopper and Clay-colored Sparrows, Wilson's Snipe, and plenty of Eastern Meadowlarks and Bobolinks. Birding along the J/I Line is best in the early morning, though grassland birds tend to be active throughout the day. The best strategy is to slowly drive the road and stop periodically in suitable grassland habitat.

At the end of the J/I Line, head west on Bruce Saugeen Townline Rd. towards the dead end at the lake. After the intersection with Lake Range Rd., MacGregor Point Provincial Park will be on your right (north). In this stretch there is some excellent early successional forest; drive slowly and stop in the shrubby, second-growth habitats, keeping a listen for the high-pitched buzzy songs of Blue-winged and Golden-winged Warblers, which should both be found here. In the more deciduous forested habitats, species like American Redstart, Mourning Warbler, and Yellow-throated Vireo are present. You might spot Sedge Wrens in the more open habitats, though they are highly variable from year to year.

As you're making your way west, keep an eye out for a large wetland on your right (north). At the far west end of the wetland you'll come to a small bridge spanning the drainage ditch that you can cross to the north side of the road into MacGregor Point Provincial Park; it leads to an observation tower over the Ducks Unlimited (DU) Ponds. Keep in mind that to enter the park you must have a valid permit, which you can buy at the park gate for a small fee. The DU Ponds are excellent in the breeding season, with a good selection of typical marsh birds including Virginia Rail, Sora, and Least Bittern. Often we like to linger here, with early morning or dusk being the best times. Back at the road, continue west to the lake. There are several spots here to park and scan the shoreline for waterbirds at any time of the year, and birding the road for migrant forest birds can be productive.

Once you've checked the lake, backtrack to Lake Range Rd. and travel north along the eastern perimeter of MacGregor Point Provincial Park. The first 300 m/yds of the road can be good for Sedge Wren and Alder Flycatcher, while from there to 1.3 km (0.8 mi.) can be good for Chestnut-sided, Golden-winged, and Blue-winged Warblers and Indigo Buntings. The area around the main park entrance provides rich deciduous forest, with typical species being Great Crested Flycatcher, Scarlet Tanager, Eastern Wood-Pewee, and Pileated Woodpecker. On summer nights this area, as well as the campground, typically has Eastern Whip-poor-wills and the odd Eastern Screech-Owl calling throughout.

From MacGregor Point head north on Hwy. 21, through Port Elgin and Southampton, and continue up CR 13 to Sauble Beach. This is the last spot that we typically check in southern Bruce County. Since 2007, Sauble Beach has been the best location in the province for Piping Plovers, no small thanks to the hard work of the plover volunteers. Over the last five years or so, typically 1–3 pairs nest here; the best location to check for them is at the mouth of the Sauble River on the south side. In the breeding season, plover volunteers are present and always very helpful in locating the birds if asked. At the beach you should be able to see from a long way away the nest exclosure (a cage over the nest to prevent predation) and the habitat fence around the general area of any nests.

GETTING THERE

The region is easily accessed from Hwy. 21 and Hwy. 9 and is situated an hour and 45 minutes from Kitchener-Waterloo in good driving conditions. In winter the area receives a significant amount of snow, being in the "snowbelt," so check the local forecast before departing, take your time, and be prepared for serious winter driving conditions.

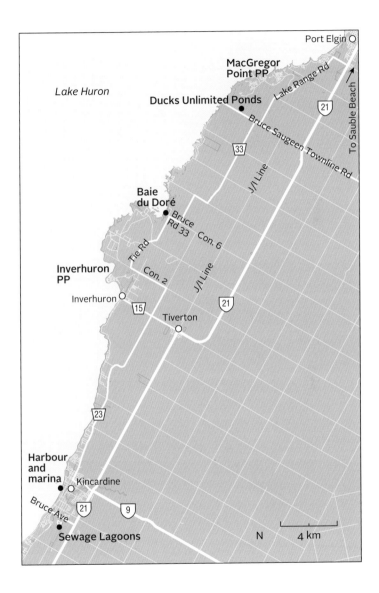

Port Elgin

MacGregor
Point PP

Lake Huron

Ducks Unlimited Ponds

Lake Range Rd

21

To Sauble Beach

Bruce Saugeen Townline Rd

33

J/I Line

Baie
du Doré

Bruce
Rd 33 · Con. 6

Tie Rd

Con. 2

J/I Line

Inverhuron
PP

Inverhuron

15

21

Tiverton

23

Harbour
and
marina

Kincardine

Bruce Ave

21

9

N   4 km

Sewage Lagoons

10

PORT STANLEY TO PORT BURWELL

OVERVIEW

Originally an important route for European explorers in the 17th and 18th centuries, the coastline from Port Stanley to Port Burwell is best known today for its tourism and recreational fishing. For birders, though, the area is host to an epic fall hawk migration that starts in late August and runs through early December, with its peak from mid-September through mid-October. The region is located within the equally significant, yet not as well known, Norfolk Sand Plain and has a relatively high proportion of forest cover by southern Ontario standards.

◀ The north shore of Lake Erie in late fall is among eastern North America's top areas to see Golden Eagles migrating south; perhaps no other location is as famous for them in Ontario as Hawk Cliff. BRANDON HOLDEN

One of the most famous birding locations in the province is Hawk Cliff, in the western part of this region. It's known as one of the premier hawk-watching spots in North America and observers have recorded over 100,000 birds of prey in a single day! Typical daily numbers at this site are obviously much lower, but a few times each fall, on days with northwest winds following the passage of cold fronts, it is not unusual to see as many as 7,500 raptors.

Located at the east end of this region lies Port Burwell, a quaint town roughly 15 km (9 mi.) west of the Long Point peninsula. Despite there being few field observers, a remarkable host of rarities have turned up here: Black-tailed Gull, Black-throated Gray Warbler, Black-throated Sparrow, and Eurasian Tree Sparrow, to name a few in the past decade alone. Excellent waterbird concentrations occur along the shoreline and, in particular, at the mouth of Big Otter Creek and the beach of Port Burwell Provincial Park. Passerines are well represented, with excellent diversity and numbers found during both spring and fall migrations.

Summer is generally slower; however, many of the quintessential Carolinian breeders are found here, such as Louisiana Waterthrush, Cerulean, Hooded, and Blue-winged Warblers, Yellow-billed Cuckoo, and Acadian Flycatcher, to name a few.

BIRDING STRATEGY

From the centre of Port Stanley, head northwest on Carlow Rd., Lake Line, and Scotch Line until you reach the Port Stanley Sewage Lagoons; here you'll find a series of four cells, with two viewing blinds. The water level in the sewage lagoons is generally high; however, the waterfowl are typically diverse and abundant, with a variety of diving and dabbling ducks.

Tundra Swans pass through in decent numbers in mid-to-late March, while there are good numbers of Ruddy and Wood Ducks, along with both species of teal, from mid-April into September. When water levels are low, the cells can be productive for shorebirds. On one memorable visit during a torrential downpour, we found the edges of the near cell lined with dozens of Short-billed Dowitchers. Shorebirding is best from mid-May through early June and again from late July through September.

Continuing from the sewage lagoons back to the town of Port Stanley, check the town beach on the west side of Kettle Creek. You'll often see a wide variety of waterbirds, as well as shorebirds. Make sure to scan the lake and any gull flocks on the beach, as Little and Lesser Black-backed as well as white-winged gulls (Glaucous Gull, and Kumlien's and Thayer's subspecies of Iceland Gull) can be present at any time of the year, though predominantly in late fall to early spring. On the east side of Kettle Creek is the harbour: it's worth scanning the breakwall for gulls and shorebirds, while the inner harbour is a good location for Horned Grebe in spring and fall migration. Late May in particular can have resting flocks of Whimbrel or other shorebirds, like Ruddy Turnstone and Sanderling. In late fall, be sure to scan through lingering Turkey Vultures for the much rarer Black Vulture.

As you head east from Port Stanley on County Road (CR) 24 (Dexter Line), no stop in this area is complete until you've checked out Hawk Cliff by heading south on Hawk Cliff Rd. This spot is best known for the fall raptor migration, but in the summer it's worth checking the wooded ravine along the road, about halfway from Dexter Line to the lake, for Acadian Flycatchers—they regularly nest here. A crowd of hawk watchers usually gathers at the far south end of Hawk Cliff Rd. during fall migration (September 1 to late November), particularly on clear days with northwest winds following a cold front. We generally find it easiest to spot birds when there's some cloud cover. The wooded areas adjacent to the viewing area can also be great for passerines during spring and fall migrations, and observers regularly see 20+ species of warblers here in a day.

Moving east along CR 24 to Port Bruce, we recommend checking the town itself, particularly the lakeshore. Gulls and shorebirds can be present along the beach (Port Bruce Provincial Park) and ducks may be in the river mouth (Catfish Creek); have a quick look and move on if you don't see much at either spot. North of Port Bruce is the Yarmouth Natural Heritage Area, located along Sparta Line just 2.8 km (1.7 mi.) east of Sparta and operated by the Catfish Creek Conservation Authority. To get there from Port Bruce, zig-zag north and west, taking Rush Creek Line, Jamestown Line, Roberts Line, and Chestnut Grove Rd. to Sparta Line, where a small parking lot is located just east of Catfish Creek. The natural area is especially productive during the breeding season, with Cerulean and Hooded Warblers along with Louisiana Waterthrush, while more northern species such as Black-and-white Warbler are also here. The constructed wetland within the property provides good numbers of Willow Flycatchers and Swamp Sparrows. Driving the roads slowly between Port Bruce and the Yarmouth Natural Heritage Area should produce a good assortment of Carolinian breeders too, such as Yellow-billed Cuckoos and Blue-winged Warblers.

From Port Bruce, head east along the lakeshore to Port Burwell on Imperial Rd. and Nova Scotia Line/CR 42. In Port

Burwell, the public beach south of the downtown area is a great place to start. Gulls, terns, and shorebirds typically loaf on the beach, while waterbirds are present offshore. A number of rarities have shown up here, not to mention the fact that it's very consistent for species like Common and Forster's Terns, as well as Bonaparte's and Little Gulls (particularly in July).

On the west side of Big Otter Creek via Chatham St. lies Port Burwell Provincial Park. The park itself is a gem, offering good camping and birding. It's also a great location that few birders seem to go to, despite the large number of rarities found here. Spring and fall passerine migration can be excellent, and the park itself can be just as good as the other better-known migrant traps along the north shore of Lake Erie. When you arrive at the entrance, obtain a park pass at the gate. We'd recommend parking here and walking along the edge of the mowed areas. Following this strategy, you'll reach several beach-access points that are worth checking. When walking through the dunes, keep an eye out: there are often good numbers of sparrows in migration. Along the lake, waterbirds are often present in good numbers, particularly gulls in late summer and fall. We hope the beach will host nesting Piping Plovers in the near future, as the habitat is great.

Driving the shoreline from Port Stanley to Port Burwell in winter can produce some of the best winter birding in the province, with large numbers of sparrows and other lingering species, like Red-shouldered Hawks and blackbirds. This is a favourite outing of ours, especially in early January, when we want to boost our year list total quickly. For lingering species, focus on highly sheltered ravines. We like to check this area after a good snowfall, when many lingering birds take advantage of snowplow-cleared patches on roads.

GETTING THERE

Reach Port Stanley by exiting Hwy. 401 at Union Rd./Elgin Rd. 20 (exit 164) and heading south. Take Union Rd. all the way into Port Stanley. Alternatively, head south from St. Thomas on Sunset Dr./Hwy. 4 until you reach Port Stanley.

To get to Port Bruce, take Dexter Line/CR 24 east for 16 km (10 mi.). Once in Port Bruce, turn right (south) on Imperial Rd./Regional Road 73. Imperial Rd. ends at a turnaround.

Port Burwell can be reached by continuing south from Tillsonburg on CR 19 for 20 km (12.4 mi.) through Straffordville and Vienna.

PORT STANLEY

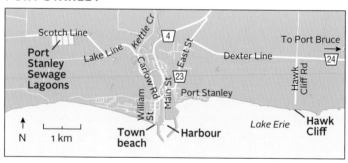

PORT BRUCE

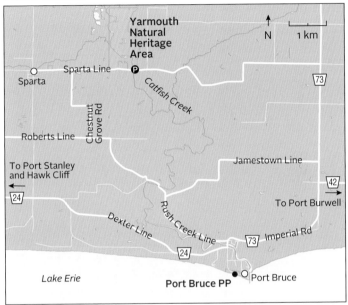

PORT BURWELL

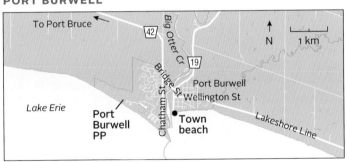

The Long Point region is the stronghold for Hooded Warblers in Canada, with over 100 pairs present! Look and listen for them in any of the area woodlots.
MICHAEL BURRELL

11

LONG POINT, PORT ROWAN

OVERVIEW

Long Point looms large on the list of birding sites the province has to offer. If a birder from outside Ontario has heard of any sites in this book, it will likely be this one and/or Point Pelee (Chapter 3). That fame is well founded, as the Long Point area boasts a checklist of over 400 species and has probably the most significant concentration of birds in the entire province.

The Long Point area is dominated by the massive point itself—at over 30 km (18 mi.), it's touted as the longest fresh-water sand spit in the world. The point forms Long Point Bay—a shallow, rich water body. Big Creek Marsh, at the base of the point, is one of the largest freshwater marshes left in the province, and the marshes at Turkey Point and on Long Point are also very large. The mainland at first glance is typical of southwestern Ontario—a mostly rural area with intensive agriculture. However, because of reforestation efforts, the forest cover is higher here than in almost any other part of southern Ontario that's not underlain by the Canadian Shield. It includes some of the largest remaining tracts of Carolinian forest (southern deciduous forest) in the province.

Besides agriculture, Port Rowan—the mainland town serving Long Point—has become a growing retirement community, and the community of Long Point itself is home mostly to seasonal cottagers who enjoy the huge expanse of beautiful sand beach in the summer. As well, Long Point has an extremely long history of ornithological research and is home to the Long Point Bird Observatory (LPBO) and its parent organization, Bird Studies Canada (BSC). LPBO was established in 1960 by the Ontario Bird Banding Association, whose members had been periodically fitting birds on the point with numbered leg bands. They set up a banding station at the very tip of the point, followed later by a station about a third of the way out ("Breakwater") and another one at the base of the point ("Old Cut"). The two stations on the point are not accessible to the public, but Old Cut welcomes visitors.

Birding at Long Point has a special place in our hearts because, as kids, we first learned about professional birders by volunteering at LPBO and BSC. What had been a hobby became a passion as we built countless Barn Owl and Prothonotary Warbler nest boxes for recovery programs run by BSC and spent our summers volunteering at LPBO. Long Point offers excellent birding at all times of the year, and you can easily spend weeks exploring all of the birding spots it has to offer. If you plan to spend a lot of time here, pick up a copy of Ron

Ridout's *A Birding Guide to the Long Point Area*—copies should be available at the BSC headquarters store or LPBO's Old Cut banding station.

BIRDING STRATEGY

If you're here during the breeding season, your best bet is to head for the inland woodlots. There are several large forests in the area, but the most productive for the Carolinian specialties is Backus Woods. Be warned that after conducting fieldwork all over the province, including the tundra and boreal forests of northern Ontario, we can confirm that the mosquitoes of Long Point's woodlots in June are some of the most ferocious we've ever encountered—bring your bug spray and don't even think about shorts! From Port Rowan, head north on Hwy. 59 and follow it to Concession 3. Turn right, watching for the historical plaque commemorating the Wild Turkey reintroduction. Turn left at the Wild Turkey plaque and follow the narrow laneway to a small parking lot. Backus Woods is bordered by Concession 3 on the south and Hwy. 24 on the north, with Concession 4 cutting right through the middle. You can access it from any of those roads and walk the trails in loops or straight through.

The area around the turkey cairn is good for Blue-winged Warbler, Field Sparrow, Eastern Towhee, and occasionally other shrub species like White-eyed Vireo and Golden-winged Warbler. Walk the trail to the north, into the deciduous forest, and you'll immediately be in Louisiana Waterthrush territory—several individuals nest in the wooded sloughs here. Crossing Concession 4 or driving up and parking here, there's another trail heading north (be sure to access from the west, as Concession 4 is usually not passable east of the trails). Follow the vehicle track trail north, keeping an ear out for Hooded Warbler, Louisiana Waterthrush, and Acadian Flycatcher as you go. When you get to the pond on your right (east), listen (and look) low around the pond for the ringing *zweet-zweeet-zweeet-zweeet* of the Prothonotary Warbler and in the treetops for the Cerulean Warbler. Exploring all of the trails of Backus Woods should give you a good shot at spotting all of these species and many more that nest here.

At most other times of year you're best to start at the Old Cut research station (LPBO's public banding station) by heading south on Hwy. 59 from Port Rowan. This road will take you across the Long Point Causeway before turning sharply left (east) at the Long Point townsite. Just before you reach Long Point Provincial Park at the end of the road, turn left (north) onto Old Cut Blvd. After seven or eight houses on your left will be a large (free) parking lot. Park here and walk across the street to the field station. During songbird migration (April 1 to June 10 and mid-August to mid-November), daily banding takes place each morning (weather permitting) so you can literally take a seat and have the birds brought to you! You'll also want to check the sightings board here and talk to the banders to find out what species are around. If you're here in winter, check behind the banding lab for birds at the feeders—there are often lingering sparrows and the odd blackbird. When you're ready to head out, explore the trails in the Old Cut woodlot and stroll down Lighthouse Cres. towards Long Point Provincial Park. Virtually anywhere here can be absolutely hopping with birds, and more than 325 species have been observed at Old Cut alone!

If you have time, a walk through Long Point Provincial Park can also be very productive. If it's windy, bird the leeward side of the treed areas. When we were teenagers here during spring migration, we would usually ride our bicycles to the far end of the park and bird around the playground area as it always seemed to have something to offer—including, on one occasion, our lifer (first) Cerulean Warbler hopping on the ground. Checking the beach is always worthwhile for gulls and shorebirds—two separate Snowy Plovers have turned up here, including one Ken found just after Mike had left (before we had cellphones). The marshes along the north edge of the park can also be very good for rails, ducks, and herons.

Head back west along Hwy. 59. If you're here in winter, driving the cottage roads looking for houses with feeders can be productive. In migration, stopping anywhere can turn up flocks of sparrows and warblers. Where the road bends sharply north is Hastings Dr. on your left. This road can be impassable depending on conditions, so take care here. Surrounded by beach and lake to the south and Big Creek Marsh to the north, the entire road cuts through a narrow strip of trees and can be a great birding spot. It is one of our absolute favourites. Checking feeders here may turn up rarities, and walking the whole road or stretches of it is productive at most times of the year.

Head back to Hwy. 59 and go north onto the Long Point Causeway. There's a viewing stand on the right, just as you pass the marina, that is an important vantage from which to scan the Inner Bay (scope recommended). During the breeding season, you'll see Forster's Tern colonies and the birds will be in constant view foraging over the bay or marsh. The number of ducks here can be truly impressive, as are the big flocks of Tundra Swans when they're around. There may also be the odd Little Gull.

A bit farther up the road on the left is the parking lot for the Big Creek National Wildlife Area. There's a viewing platform here too that offers great views of the marsh laid out before you to the west. During the breeding season, it's worth walking the loop trail, particularly at dawn or dusk, as marsh birds are in full song. The sounds of Virginia Rails, Soras, Sandhill Cranes, and American and Least Bitterns are all fairly common here. The occasional King Rail will also be heard grunting away. A bit farther north is the bridge over Big Creek—it's worth stopping and scanning here as well. When most of the bay is frozen, this is the first area to open (and the last to freeze) so ducks and swans can often be packed in, including lingering Pied-billed Grebes and Wood Ducks in winter.

Continue north on Hwy. 59. If you have time, you might want to do a small loop to the west, especially during waterfowl migration. Head west on County Road (CR) 42 (Lakeshore Rd.) and watch the fields for Tundra Swans and Sandhill Cranes. The first dip on the right (1 km/0.6 mi.) is particularly good for flocks of waterfowl and cranes. Just past Port Royal you'll come to Lee Brown Waterfowl Management Area, which is basically a dug-out pond beside the road that can be absolutely packed with ducks and geese. Rarities like Eurasian Wigeon and Greater White-fronted Goose are seen here almost annually. You can keep driving down CR 42 looking for flocks of swans and cranes, or you can turn around.

Head back towards Port Rowan and just after you cross the small creek you'll see the BSC headquarters on your right.

Walking trails through the field lead back to a viewing deck overlooking Inner Bay. The view is spectacular and can sometimes include tens of thousands of ducks and thousands of swans. As you walk the trail along the back edge, look for migrant songbirds. If you continue west along the shore, you'll reach the cemetery, where you can walk up the road and complete a loop around the wetland. The pond has had nesting Least Bitterns as well as a good selection of ducks, shorebirds, and even some rarities like Little Blue Herons and Yellow-headed Blackbirds.

Continue into Port Rowan and stop at the constructed wetland by turning left onto Hunter Dr.—the wetland is located 500 m/yds ahead on your right. It's great for Common Gallinule from late April to September and often hosts a good assortment of dabbling ducks. Shorebirds are possible if the water levels are low.

Head back to Lakeshore Rd. and turn left to continue into Port Rowan. Stop at Long Point (Port Rowan) Lions Park (on your right, just as the road curves north to downtown) for another vantage out to the Inner Bay. Scan the bay for ducks and Little Gulls—the North American record of 266 was set here on November 6, 1988. Take the first right onto Wolven St. (which turns into Front Rd.) and follow it through the jog at the town of St. Williams all the way to Turkey Point Rd. In winter, driving along Front Rd. can be productive for roadside sparrows and blackbird flocks. During migration, flocks of Tundra Swans are often overhead.

Head south on Turkey Point Rd. to the T-junction and turn right. Follow this road to the marina or any one of the beach-access points. Start by searching the beach for shorebirds and then scan through the ducks out on the lake. This site is also one of the most reliable in North America for large numbers of Little Gulls. March through May and October to November are peak times for this species.

GETTING THERE

Long Point, despite being in southwestern Ontario, is actually a long way from most places. If you're coming from the Toronto area, head west on Hwy. 403 through Hamilton towards Brantford and then exit onto Hwy. 6. Turn right onto St. Johns Road (CR 3) before you get to Port Dover and then turn left at the traffic lights onto Hwy. 24. Follow Hwy. 24 all the way to the stop sign at Hwy. 59 and head south until you reach the intersection with CR 42. If you're coming from the west, get off Hwy. 401 at exit 218 and follow CR 19 into Tillsonburg. In town, go east on CR 3 for about 7 km (4 mi.) before heading south on Hwy. 59. Follow this road to CR 42 at Port Rowan.

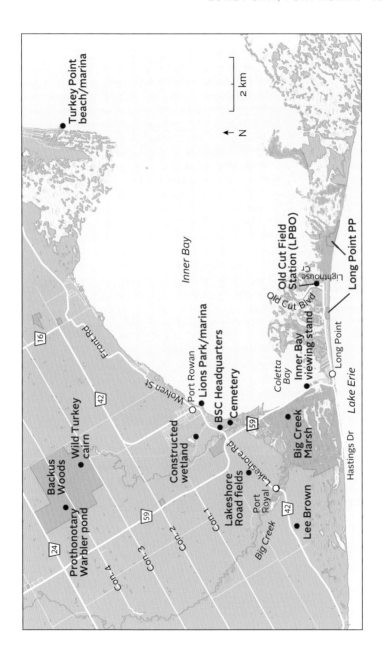

With varying amounts of black in their outer wing tips, Iceland Gulls are regularly seen along the Niagara River. BRANDON HOLDEN

12
NIAGARA RIVER

OVERVIEW

Niagara Falls is easily one of the most popular tourist destinations in Canada. What most tourists don't know, though, is that the Niagara River is also one of the best locations in the world for gull watching. From Lake Erie, the river travels approximately 58 km (36 mi.) to Lake Ontario, where it discharges roughly one-third the volume of the Mississippi River—that's a lot of water! Because of the high discharge rates, the water is open year-round, which means lots of food for gulls and other waterbirds. Eighteen species of gulls have been observed along the river—a total that few places in the world can rival.

The river as a whole is identified as an Important Bird and Biodiversity Area (IBA) largely because of the huge concentration of gulls. More than 40,000 Bonaparte's, 50,000 Herring, and 20,000 Ring-billed Gulls have been counted along the river, and the area regularly plays host to rarer gulls, with records of Slaty-backed, Ross's, Mew, and California Gulls here. Peak gull season is mid-November to mid-December, which is also the quiet season for general tourists, so birders often enjoy excellent rates on local hotels and fewer crowds than at other times of the year. In addition to gulls, the river is also excellent for wintering Canvasbacks and Greater Scaups, with continentally significant counts being recorded here.

Birders visiting the province at any time of the year, though particularly in winter, will want to visit Niagara. In recent years, both Fish Crows and Black Vultures have seemingly become established here, and though there have been no confirmed reports of nesting, it seems only a matter of time before this occurs. Several other species are relatively common here, yet uncommon elsewhere in Ontario: Tufted Titmouse, Red-bellied Woodpecker, Carolina Wren, and Northern Mockingbird all have their provincial strongholds in this region. Overall, we recommend visiting in winter, though the river can be exciting and productive at any time of the year.

BIRDING STRATEGY
Given its length, the Niagara River has far too many locations to check than can be covered here. Below, we've laid out our favourite spots in four sections along a north–south gradient: Niagara-on-the-Lake, Queenston, the falls, and Fort Erie. If you're looking for waterbirds, a scope is pretty much essential as the birds can be far away from shore.

The Niagara River is one of the world's best locations for gulls, with close to 20 species observed. JEAN IRON

Niagara-on-the-Lake. Within the quaint town of Niagara-on-the-Lake, we typically check two locations: Queen's Royal Park and Fort George National Historic Site. Both spots overlook the river mouth, and we like to visit them at the end of the day to watch the flypast—when the gulls on the river fly out to roost on Lake Ontario for the night. This is a sure bet to see hundreds and routinely thousands of Bonaparte's Gulls flying steadily by, and a great way to look for rarities among them. Careful observers regularly see several Little Gulls and, on rarer occasions, Black-headed Gulls too.

From downtown, take Regent St. north; the parking lot for Queen's Royal Park will be on the opposite side of Front St. Queen's Royal Park is an elevated location that provides a great view (scope recommended!) of the river mouth. In winter, you can expect to find Red-throated and Common Loons and Horned and Red-necked Grebes, along with all three species of scoters and good numbers of Long-tailed Ducks. In fall, this location can be a good place to watch the lake for Pomarine and Parasitic Jaegers. The river mouth is also a magnet for Razorbills, hosting four different birds over the years!

Travelling south on Ricardo St. for 1 km (0.6 mi.), you'll reach Fort George. It provides another good view of the river, on the south side of Niagara-on-the-Lake. It is more sheltered from wind than Queen's Royal Park, and in winter it can be much more pleasant to view the river from here.

Queenston. The Queenston area provides several great locations to check along the river. Start with the Queenston boat docks, which you reach by taking Dumfries St. east from the Niagara Pkwy. and crossing Princess St. before descending the escarpment. Drive slowly down the hill as it is very steep. A good number of gulls are usually feeding over the water here. Scanning from the boat docks is a good strategy to look for Little Gulls and any other interesting gulls that are around in late fall and winter.

Travel back to the Niagara Pkwy. and continue south, up the escarpment. Just before the sharp bend is a pull-off that overlooks the river from an elevated vantage. Make sure you stop here and scan the river with a scope. This is the best spot to search for Black Vultures—often there are several with a group of Turkey Vultures on the American side, though they regularly fly back and forth. While you're scoping the vultures, check the wooded slopes for Carolina Wren and Red-bellied Woodpecker.

Continue south along the parkway, and just after you pass under the Queenston-Lewiston Bridge you'll see a pull-off parking area for the Adam Beck Generating Station on your left. Don't be fooled into thinking that this spot couldn't possibly produce excellent birds—in fact, it is likely the top spot on the river, partly because the generating station churns up the water, aquatic invertebrates, and small fish, creating a buffet that only gulls could love! Scoping from the edge of the parking lot and looking down should yield Iceland (both Kumlien's and Thayer's), Glaucous, and Lesser Black-backed Gulls among the hordes of Herring and Bonaparte's Gulls. Some years, Harlequin Ducks have overwintered here, so make sure to scope down the river on either side of the generating plant. Keep an eye out for vultures as well, as Blacks sometimes show up this far away from Queenston. There are some large flat rocks about 500 m/yds south of the parking lot that often host roosting gulls. You can easily walk the trail from the parking area and scope the river and rocks, where large numbers of resting gulls usually congregate, particularly in the afternoon. In recent years most species have been the same as at the power plant, but there have also been Franklin's and California Gulls.

Driving south along the parkway, keep an eye out for Northern Mockingbirds along the roadside in small bushes at any time of the year. After 5 km (3 mi.) you'll come across another parking lot to view the Whirlpool. If the tourists don't scare you away, be sure to scope the river; usually, a thousand or two Bonaparte's Gulls are feeding below, with the odd Little or even Black-headed Gull thrown into the mix.

The Falls. We don't usually spend as much time here as other birders we know, but checking below the falls can be productive. This can be an especially good spot for interesting overwintering waterbirds (like loons and grebes), along with good gulls. Several Ross's Gulls have shown up here over the years, including one that Ken found as a teen. To park, we usually continue south, past the falls, to a free parking lot at the Dufferin Islands. From there, we walk back north towards the falls, spending some time checking out the river along the way.

The old building above the falls is known as the pumphouse, and good views can be had of the rocks from above and below this building. Scanning the rocks is a good strategy for finding Lesser Black-backed Gulls and white-winged gulls (Iceland and Glaucous) and sometimes Little Gulls. In recent years, several Harlequin Ducks have overwintered in the river around the barge, while common wintering ducks here generally include Gadwall, Common Goldeneye, Bufflehead, and the odd Hooded Merganser. Make sure to carefully check each rock for Purple Sandpipers too, though they can be tough to see. In summer, keep an eye out for the resident pair of Peregrine Falcons and scan the islands in the river, as Great Egrets and Black-crowned Night-Herons are usually present.

Once you've had your fill of the falls area, walk back through Dufferin Islands and make sure to check the chickadee flocks for Tufted Titmice—they will often hand-feed if you've brought food for them. A few hundred metres south of Dufferin Islands are the control gates, which regulate the flow of water for hydroelectric power generation. We generally just park in the small pull-off here and scope the river and breakwall. When the water is low, hundreds of large gulls will loaf on the breakwall, allowing for easy study. California, Slaty-backed, and Mew Gulls have been found here in recent years. Several islands are located in the middle of the river, providing another spot where gulls loaf, though they're farther away. Hundreds of ducks should be present too, with large numbers of Common Goldeneye and Bufflehead closer to shore and in the fast sections of water. Above the control gates we typically find decent-sized flocks of Greater Scaup, Redhead, and Canvasback, along with small scattered groups of Tundra Swans.

Fort Erie. Located about 24 km (15 mi.) from the control gates is the northern edge of Fort Erie. You can take a scenic drive along the Niagara Pkwy. and spot lots of waterfowl along the river, but generally the gulls are concentrated around the Queenston and falls areas. Often we find that the best strategy is to head for Fort Erie and stop periodically to scan the river, especially if we see large groups of birds. The area around

Bowen Rd. and the railway bridge has been good for Fish Crows in the past several years—watch for any large flocks of crows and listen for their nasal *uh-uh* calls as they hang out with their American cousins. Checking the large Bonaparte's Gull flocks here can pay off, with Black-headed and Sabine's Gulls and Black-legged Kittiwakes showing up regularly. Other places to check include the Peace Bridge, Mather Park, and the Old Fort parking lot. These locations, while excellent in winter, can also be good in spring and fall for waterfowl, with excellent numbers of Greater Scaups, Buffleheads, and Canvasbacks.

The last spot we've included in this chapter is Waverly Beach just past Fort Erie. Located at the end of Helena St., Waverly Beach has had fantastic rarities over the years and is a highly underbirded location, especially on strong southwesterly winds in the fall. Given the shape of Lake Erie, southwesterly winds will literally blow the entire length of the lake, bringing pelagics close to shore. Post-hurricane winds have brought in extreme rarities; however, even watching the lake under normal conditions can produce good birds, with all three jaegers, Black-legged Kittiwakes, Sabine's Gulls, and Red Phalaropes, among others. It wouldn't be a stretch to consider Waverly Beach the Van Wagner's (Chapter 14) of Lake Erie.

GETTING THERE

The Niagara River is easily accessed from the Queen Elizabeth Way (QEW) and Hwy. 405. It is an easy 35-minute drive from Hamilton. All the birding sites can be reached from the Niagara Pkwy., which runs the length of the river from end to end.

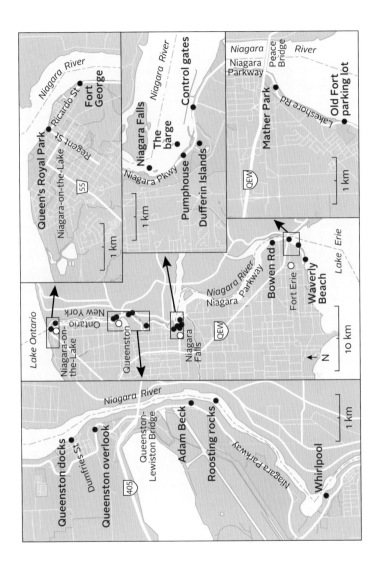

Flocks of scoters, like this group of male Surfs, are a regular sight along the Lake Ontario shoreline in winter. BRANDON HOLDEN

13

STONEY CREEK–
GRIMSBY SHORELINE

OVERVIEW

The narrow strip of land sandwiched between the south shore
of Lake Ontario and the steep wooded slopes of the Niagara
Escarpment may seem like an unlikely place to bird. After
all, the city of Hamilton has spread east along the shoreline
from the end of the lake through what was once the separate
town of Stoney Creek. Nearby Grimsby has expanded both
east and west along the lake. And just beyond is the rest of
Niagara Region. Among the developments and the farmland
are a few scattered parks along the lakeshore that offer good
vantages for scanning the lake and, if there are trees, good
opportunities for observing migrant landbirds.

This area makes up one part of the West End of Lake
Ontario Important Bird and Biodiversity Area (IBA), which

runs from the mouth of the Niagara River all the way to Mississauga on the north shore of the lake. More than 1% of the global population of Common Goldeneyes, Greater Scaups, Long-tailed Ducks, White-winged Scoters, and Red-breasted Mergansers have visited the nearshore waters here in migration or in winter, and observers regularly count in the multiple thousands of all these species. The draw of this area is certainly the waterbirds that concentrate here. In fact, it is probably the best place in the province to see all three scoters and King Eiders while scanning the huge flocks of ducks on the lake from fall through spring. During spring and fall migrations, the number of landbirds concentrated in the lakeshore woodlots can be impressive here too. And this is the prime spot in Ontario to observe spring raptor migration as the birds follow the escarpment west.

We regularly combine birding in this area with birding the sites in Hamilton Harbour (Chapter 14), and we always visit some of these sites on our way to the Niagara River (Chapter 12).

BIRDING STRATEGY

During the spring raptor migration (March to early May), it's worth keeping your eyes peeled at all times. In particular, heading to Beamer Memorial Conservation Area is an excellent bet for seeing migrant raptors overhead. To get there, exit the Queen Elizabeth Way (QEW) at exit 71 and turn right (south) onto Christie St. Follow this street "up the mountain" (don't laugh, this is apparently what qualifies as a mountain in Ontario and it's the term the locals use) and then turn right onto Ridge Rd. Drive another 1.6 km (1 mi.) until you reach Quarry Rd. and turn right. There's a small parking lot ahead on the right. That driveway leads to a clearing with an observation tower in the middle, where the spring hawk watch is conducted.

The best days for spring hawk flights are the ones following a warm front when there's a wind with a southerly component. Late March to early April brings peak numbers of many species, such as Red-shouldered Hawks and Turkey Vultures, followed by a big push of Broad-winged Hawks around mid-April. Overhead, you might also see other daytime migrants, like flocks of Tundra Swans and early swallows. At this time of year, keep watch at the feeders on the edge of the clearing for sparrows and other early migrants. In summer, the woods can be productive for forest birds, including Pileated Woodpecker and Eastern Wood-Pewee. At other times of year, you'll probably want to concentrate on sites directly along the lakeshore.

To get back to the lake, retrace your route to Ridge Rd., turn right (west) and continue for 2 km (1.2 mi.). Turn right (north) onto Woolverton Rd. and follow it until the T-junction. Turn left (west) onto Main St. for 2.4 km (1.5 mi.) and then right (north) on Oakes Rd., which leads over the QEW to end at Winston Rd. Go left (west) on this road for 200 m/yds and you'll arrive at the small parkette for the decommissioned Grimsby/Biggar Sewage Lagoons. The ponds here are great for ducks and herons, and if the water levels are low (most likely in late summer), the ponds can attract a good selection of shorebirds. It's also worth checking the shrubs around the edge of the ponds for migrant warblers and sparrows.

A little farther west, just past the point where Winston Rd. becomes Baseline Rd., is Fifty Point Conservation Area.

Turn right into the parking lot, pay the entrance fee at the gate (you can also get an annual pass online), and follow the trails towards the lake. (Alternatively, you can turn right a bit earlier, at Kelson Ave., drive to the north end of the street, and then walk to the beach.) The walk out to the beach can be excellent for migrant landbirds in season but the draw, of course, is the viewing area at the top of the small rise to your north. This vantage point is an excellent one for scanning the lake for rafts of ducks as well as other waterbirds. Northern Gannets have been seen here on several occasions along with all three jaegers. In late fall and early winter, check the boulders along the water's edge for Purple Sandpipers. County listers should take note that the boundary between Niagara and Hamilton is approximately the mouth of the marina—everything to the west is in Hamilton and to the east is Niagara. Exploring the rest of Fifty Point can yield pockets of warblers, vireos, and flycatchers during migration, and in winter the conifers are a good place to search for roosting owls. It's also worth checking the pond in the interior of the property for ducks and herons from spring through fall.

When Baseline Rd. ends, turn left onto Lockport Way and then immediately right (west) to get back onto North Service Rd. Keep heading west on North Service, taking any opportunity you can to scan the lake from the numerous dead-end roads to your right (north). From fall through spring, periodically scanning the lake is the best strategy to find the large duck rafts as their location changes daily. You won't have any problem finding Long-tailed Ducks (often in the tens of thousands), but it can be trickier to find the flocks of scoters. If you do find them, scan carefully—the King Eiders that overwinter are often mixed in with these flocks. Also keep an eye out for Barrow's Goldeneye (rarer) and Harlequin Duck, both of which are present along the shoreline nearly annually. Some of our favourite vantage points, from east to west, are at the ends of Fruitland, Dewitt, and Millen Rds.

West of Millen Rd. is Green Rd., which is marked by several large residential towers along the lake. The end of this road is often one of the best places to scan the lake for ducks, and we almost never drive by without at least a quick check.

Instead of heading back to North Service Rd. from here, go right (west) on Frances Ave. and you'll come to Edgelake Park. This wooded park may be small, but in migration it can be mighty—a whopping 34 species of warblers alone have been recorded here, including Worm-eating, Kirtland's, and Yellow-throated! So if you're in the area during April to May or August to October, it is definitely worth the short walk to see lots of interesting songbirds.

From the park, continue west on Frances Ave. to Drakes Dr. Turn right on Drakes and then right again on Lakegate Dr. to reach L.P. Sayers Park. The park may not look like much, but the vantage over the lake is excellent. We regularly enjoy all three species of scoters, and some of the highest counts of Black Scoter in southern Ontario have been made here.

Take Drakes Dr. back to North Service Rd. and go right (west). Stay on North Service as it crosses the bottom of Centennial Pkwy., where it turns into Van Wagners Beach Rd. The road makes a 90-degree turn to the right so you are heading for the lake. Just before the beach and another 90-degree turn (this time to the left) there is a small parking lot on the east side for the Waterfront Trail, which leads to

Confederation Park. Park here. The park can be busy in summer, but during migration the wooded areas can be great for landbirds—with all of the expected species in excellent numbers—and the ponds can be good for waterbirds and even shorebirds if the water levels are low. A waterfront trail runs the length of the park, providing good access to the lake for scanning as well.

Instead of driving all the way to Confederation Park, you can also access it on foot from a trail off Grays Rd. From L.P. Sayers Park, return to Drakes Dr. but turn right (west) on Frances Ave. and then right again on Grays Rd. You'll see a trailhead on your left (west) in about 100 m/yds. Starting here is often a good strategy, as some of the better birding spots are at the east end of the park.

GETTING THERE

Any spot within this entire area is only minutes from the QEW, east of Hamilton. No matter which direction you're coming from, get off the QEW at exit 71 to reach the start of this chapter. The easternmost part of the area (Beamer) is about half an hour from downtown Hamilton or about an hour in good traffic from downtown Toronto.

STONEY CREEK: CONFEDERATION PARK
TO FRUITLAND ROAD

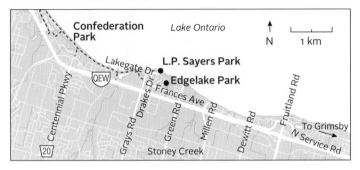

GRIMSBY: FIFTY POINT TO
BEAMER CONSERVATION AREA

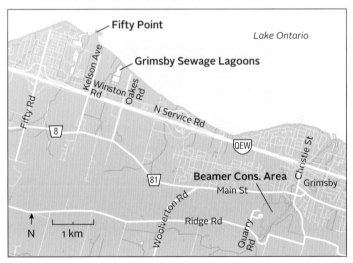

Perhaps no other location is as good as Van Wagner's Beach for seeing pelagic species that show up in fall around the Great Lakes. All three species of jaegers, like this adult Parasitic, are seen here regularly. MICHAEL BURRELL

14
HAMILTON HARBOUR

OVERVIEW

What could be more striking than a group of khaki-clad, Tilley hat–wearing birders with thousands of dollars in optical equipment staring at a pool of industrial runoff flanked by the stacks of steel manufacturing plants? While this scene plays out almost daily in and around Hamilton Harbour, you can forgive your non-birder friends for not understanding the draw of the area. Though many people have a hard time shedding the image of Hamilton—and particularly its harbour—as an industrial site, that's only part of the picture. The east side of the harbour is bounded by a thin strip of land with a long beach running along the lake. The north shore is mostly residential, and the west side is Dundas Marsh, also known as Cootes Paradise, which is surrounded primarily by the Royal

Botanical Gardens. These sites offer some of the province's top birding.

Like so many of the other best places to bird in Ontario, Hamilton Harbour offers something special at all times of the year. It's hard to pick one group of birds that the area is best known for, but if we had to, we'd say the pelagic birds visible from the beach. During fall migration, some seabirds cross overland from the Arctic Ocean via southern James Bay towards the Atlantic Ocean. This path sometimes intersects with Lake Ontario, and birds may stop and rest, particularly if they encounter poor weather. Seabirds from the Atlantic Ocean can also get pushed up the St. Lawrence River, primarily following strong east winds. Then, if winds blow from the northeast across Lake Ontario, these ocean-going birds end up at the west side of the lake—Hamilton—where birders are eagerly waiting, scopes drawn. The most frequently encountered species are jaegers, Sabine's Gull, and Black-legged Kittiwake, but the list includes Northern Gannet, storm-petrels, and even Manx Shearwater.

BIRDING STRATEGY

We generally bird this area from fall through to spring, though it is great in all seasons. Start your exploration of this area at the Van Wagners Ponds, by exiting the Queen Elizabeth Way (QEW) at exit 88. Head north to catch Van Wagners Beach Rd. and turn left (west). After a couple of 90-degree turns, the road follows closely along the beach strip. On your left are the Van Wagners Ponds. A trail that cuts through the middle of them, parallel to the road, can be an excellent place to spot a wide variety of birds during migration and occasionally in winter. Keep driving and you'll pass the famous Hutch's restaurant, a location some birders (more so in the past) use to watch the lake. A bit farther along, you'll see the tower of the Lakeland Centre.

Park at the recreational centre and head for the beach, which is now the favoured spot for lake watching on east winds as there are public washrooms nearby and interpretive signs that explain to curious passersby why you're staring out over the lake with a telescope. The prime time to see birds here runs from mid-August to early November. On days with northeast winds you can expect a small crowd of other birders. However, don't expect to just show up and see some jaegers chasing the gulls down the beach. Seeing pelagic birds requires a lot of patience, luck, and skill—the birds are often over a kilometre out. This kind of birding is not for everyone, and luckily you can leave whenever you want and check any of the other birding areas nearby.

A little past Lakeland Centre, you'll reach an intersection. Turn left onto Beach Blvd. and cross under the QEW. At the stoplights, make a right onto Eastport Dr. and, in late fall through winter, quickly pull over and park your vehicle. Just to your south, the road crosses over Red Hill Creek, which stays open all winter and is an excellent place to pick up lingering waterbirds like Double-crested Cormorants, American Coots, Northern Shovelers, and occasionally Black-crowned Night-Herons. Be sure to check both sides of the road.

Continue north on Eastport Dr. and watch for the small laneway on the left after 200 m/yds. It leads to a parking area for Windermere Basin. Park your car and walk the short trail to the viewing area. The basin has undergone a lot of habitat rehabilitation in recent years and is an excellent spot to see birds. Many of the same species seen at the Red Hill Creek bridge will also be here in winter. Since the habitat rehabilitation, however, Windermere has become excellent for shorebirds, mostly from July through September, and has fairly reliably produced uncommon species like Hudsonian Godwit and Red Knot, along with the more regular species like Black-bellied and Semipalmated Plovers and Least and Semipalmated Sandpipers. It's also worth looking for herons, as Snowy Egret has been found here several times over the last few years.

Head back to your car and turn left (west) out of the driveway back onto Eastport Dr. A bit farther along you'll see a lagoon on the left, known as the Tollgate Ponds. This area can have impressive numbers of ducks, including Ruddy Ducks and Northern Shovelers in particular, and the berms can host shorebirds in migration and are a good place to scan for Snowy Owls in winter. In summer a large colony of Ring-billed Gulls and Double-crested Cormorants is present (historically, Black-crowned Night-Herons too).

Past Tollgate Ponds you'll now have an unobstructed view of Hamilton Harbour to your left. Watch for ducks from fall through spring, and in winter large numbers of Bald Eagles and gulls (including Iceland and Glaucous) can be found on the ice. Ahead you'll cross under the QEW and you should see the Burlington lift bridge. Park in the small lot on the right, just before the bridge, and walk to the pier. Ducks are often concentrated in the channel in large numbers here, especially when the bay starts to freeze over. It can be a great place to look for King Eiders and Harlequin Ducks (be sure to walk out to the very end). However, this spot can be extremely cold in winter, so dress accordingly. While you're here, keep an eye up, as Peregrine Falcons nest on the lift bridge and are usually somewhere nearby.

Just past the lift bridge, take the left at the traffic lights and pull in to the large parking lot ahead for the Canada Centre for Inland Waters (cciw). This is a good place to scan the bay and small island for waterbirds. From here, too, you'll often see a Northern Mockingbird hanging out around the fence to the northwest. Head back to Lakeshore Rd. and then turn left (west) onto North Shore Blvd. You'll wind through a residential area for about 3.5 km (2.2 mi.) before reaching a stop sign at LaSalle Park Rd. Turn left here and park at the marina.

The docks are a popular spot for people to feed wintering ducks and, in particular, Trumpeter Swans. From fall through spring there should be a large flock of swans, and this is probably the best place in Ontario to see all three species side by side (though Tundra is usually rare). In winter it's a good place to spot less common waterbirds, so check through the birds carefully, scanning the bay in particular. Walk the small trail to the east, which can be a good place to find Carolina Wren and Tufted Titmouse year-round. It can also be good for forest birds in migration and lingering ones in winter.

Go back up LaSalle Park Rd. past North Shore Blvd. to Plains Rd. and turn left at the lights. After passing some gardens on your right, you'll see a parking area at the intersection with Botanical Dr. Pull in here and park at the far end, where a trail leads north into the forest. This trail is part of a large network that covers Hendrie Valley below. The area can be very good for winter songbirds—Carolina Wren is reliable all year.

During migration, mixed flocks of warblers and sparrows can also be found here, so it's always worth a visit.

Cross Plains Rd. on Botanical Dr. to turn right onto Spring Gardens Rd. At the end of the road is the area called Valley Inn (and access to the Grindstone Creek trail back into Hendrie Valley). This area can be good for herons and other marsh birds, as well as for migrant and wintering landbirds. Turn around to go out the way you came on Spring Gardens Rd. Ahead is Woodland Cemetery. This birding spot is one of the city's best but also the one most overlooked by out-of-towners. The southeast edge of the cemetery is on a raised bluff overlooking the harbour, which provides an excellent vantage point from which to watch birds migrating overhead. Keep an eye out for waterfowl and other diurnal migrants, including Tundra Swans, swallows, and finches in spring and fall. In fall, watch for hawk flights, particularly on northwest winds. The open wooded areas can also be excellent during migration for mixed flocks of warblers and other forest songbirds.

Continue on Spring Gardens Rd. back towards Plains Rd.—if you're hungry, stop at Easterbrook's Hotdog Stand for a snack—and head west (left). Plains Rd. curves south and becomes York Blvd. Turning right onto Old Guelph Rd. will take you to the Royal Botanical Gardens' arboretum area, where a network of trails provides access to the north shore of Cootes Paradise Marsh and fairly mature deciduous forest. This can be a good place to see Red-bellied Woodpecker and Tufted Titmouse, especially in winter, and the woods can harbour wintering and migrant landbirds like White-throated Sparrow and Winter Wren. For migrants (flocks of warblers, vireos, and sparrows in particular), we prefer the area on the south shore known as Princess Point. To get there, continue on York Blvd. and keep right onto Dundurn St. after you pass Dundurn Castle. Take another right at the first major intersection (King St.) and then right again on Macklin St. after Hwy. 403.

To get to the final location of the area, retrace your route to York Blvd. and turn right (if you skipped Princess Point, keep straight on York). Turn left onto Bay St. and then left again on Harbour Front Dr. to enter Bayfront Park. The marina and shoreline can be good areas to check for a variety of waterbirds, including Canvasbacks, Greater Scaups, and Hooded Mergansers, from fall through spring. In spring and fall, check the shrubs along the edge of the small peninsula for migrant songbirds, especially good numbers of warblers and sparrows. A waterfront trail that runs north, parallel to the shoreline, can also be excellent for migrant landbirds and has yielded some interesting lingering migrants in winter, including a fairly impressive list of warblers.

GETTING THERE

The route described here begins at exit 88 of the QEW. From Toronto, go west on the QEW and then head south towards Niagara Falls where it splits from Hwy. 403.

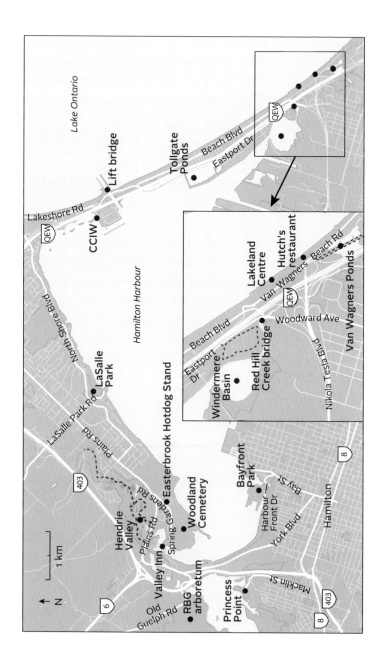

15

PEEL-HALTON SHORELINE, BURLINGTON TO MISSISSAUGA

OVERVIEW

Flying across Lake Ontario from south to north must be pretty daunting for birds. They expend all that energy to make it safely back to land, only to be met by a seemingly endless expanse of bright city lights from the Greater Toronto Area. Fortunately, a number of parks on the lake's highly urban northwestern shore offer natural features that draw large numbers of birds. Although the long, narrow stretch of shoreline from Burlington through Oakville and Mississauga to the City of Toronto is mostly occupied by residential developments, it is virtually all part of the West End of Lake Ontario Important Bird and Biodiversity Area (IBA). This area is designated for its globally significant concentrations of Long-tailed Ducks, Greater Scaups, and White-winged Scoters. It also hosts huge numbers of Red-necked Grebes each spring—over 1,000 at a single site are counted in April most years—and the total number of birds that stage here annually is in the order of 1–2% of the global population.

Many out-of-town birders know about the area's excellent waterbird scene, but most aren't aware of the abundance of small parks that are absolutely excellent for migrant forest birds in spring and fall. Days of 20+ warbler species are not uncommon in peak migration. The area is also blessed with a relatively large population of skilled birders who give great coverage to this part of the province; many rarities are found at least partly because of this thorough coverage. As such, it's always worth checking recent sightings on eBird and other channels to see what's around.

BIRDING STRATEGY

When we bird this area, we usually work our way from west to east along Lakeshore Rd., for the simple reason that we are always coming from the west. It's unlikely you'll be able to cover all of these spots in a morning, so decide where you want to start and then read on from there. Keep in mind that literally hundreds of tiny parkettes, rights-of-way, and even larger parks aren't covered here for lack of space, but all can be excellent. Don't hesitate to explore some of these additional sites while birding the area.

As a general strategy for the whole area, you should concentrate on wooded parks during songbird migration (mostly April to May and mid-August through October). From fall

Bronte Harbour is one of the only spots in southern Ontario with nesting Red-necked Grebes. Watch for impressive concentrations during peak migration in April all along the Peel-Halton shoreline. BRANDON HOLDEN

through spring the area can be very productive for ducks on the lake, including annual sightings of King Eider and Harlequin Duck. During winter months, the sheltered harbours and bays can be good places to look for winter gulls like Iceland and Glaucous Gulls. Conifers in the area can also be good places to search for wintering Long-eared and Northern Sawwhet Owls. In recent years, Fish Crows have been present in increasing numbers too, so keep an ear out for their nasally calls, mostly from March through May.

The first spot to stop at is Paletta Lakefront Park, at the foot of Shoreacres Rd. between Walkers and Appleby Lines. It's sometimes referred to by birders as Shoreacres, the name of the creek running through the eastern half of the property. The area along the creek valley is wooded with large deciduous trees while the western half of the property has scattered trees on a manicured lawn. The entire park can be excellent for migrant songbirds. As testament to this, on one memorable visit we tallied 50 species (including 15 warbler species) in under 45 minutes. Don't forget to scan the lake for waterbirds before you leave, with good numbers of all three species of scoters regularly present from fall through spring.

Farther east along Lakeshore Rd., just past Hampton Heath Rd., is Burloak Waterfront Park—another small park that can be very good for mixed flocks of migrant songbirds in season. Most of the park is manicured lawn with scattered trees, which makes searching for migrants fairly easy. There are good views out on the lake here too, and a good variety of waterbirds is generally present in season.

Not much farther along Lakeshore Rd., at the foot of Great Lakes Blvd., are South Shell Park and the Petro Canada Pier.

Again, check the strip of woods for migrant songbirds, as warblers and sparrows can be abundant and this is a fairly productive place to scan the lake. The pier can be a good spot to see Snowy Owls in winter and Purple Sandpipers in late fall and early winter. Across the road is Shell Park, a much larger park than those already mentioned. The woods are good for migrant and winter songbirds, and check the conifers for Long-eared and Northern Saw-whet Owls in winter. The area north of Shell Park used to be a woodlot called Bronte Woods that was excellent for migrant songbirds, but sadly, it has been developed for residential use.

Continuing east on Lakeshore Rd. for 2 km (1.2 mi.), you'll cross Bronte Creek. Head south down Bronte Rd. towards the lake and you'll arrive at Bronte Harbour, which is a good place to see large numbers of Red-necked Grebes during spring migration (peak in April). A pair usually nests right in the harbour, offering excellent views and photo opportunities. The park on the opposite side of the creek (Bronte Bluffs Park) is another vantage point out to the lake and can be good for migrant songbirds, particularly vireos and warblers.

Keep heading east on Lakeshore and you'll reach Third Line. Turn left (north) here and then take a right (east) on Hixon St. At the end of the road you'll be on the edge of the Sedgewick Forest. Bird the trails through the forest here for migrants in season. This forest has gained fame over the last several years as one of the best places in the province for lingering insectivores in winter. This list includes Northern Parula, as well as Tennessee, Orange-crowned, Nashville, Cape May, Bay-breasted, Palm, and Pine Warblers, all lingering into December. The reason for this concentration of birds is the presence of the Oakville Southwest Wastewater Treatment Plant smack dab in the middle of the forest. While it may be cold out, the warm, rich water provides the perfect conditions for breeding insects that emerge and provide food for these lingering species. Check the area around the perimeter of the plant in winter—this area seems to attract the most birds, though the rest of the woodlot shouldn't be forgotten.

Return to Lakeshore Rd. by taking your first left off Hixon St. onto Woodhaven Park Dr. When you reach Lakeshore, turn left (east) and drive for about 10 km (6 mi.). Just past Ford Dr. you'll come to Arkendo Park. The last wooded park before you leave the city of Oakville and Halton Region, it can again be excellent for migrant songbirds as well as lingering migrants in winter, with species like Yellow-rumped Warbler, Winter Wren, and White-throated Sparrow regularly seen here.

Back on Lakeshore Rd. and crossing east into Mississauga and the Region of Peel, Lakeside Park is just before the bend where Lakeshore Rd. becomes Southdown. The western part of the park is the most heavily treed and is the best area to check in migration for songbirds. The park is also a good place to scan the lake for waterbirds—often large flocks of scaups and scoters are present in fall through early spring.

Driving east, follow Lakeshore as it becomes Southdown Rd. and stay with it for 2.5 km (1.6 mi.) before you turn right to get back onto Lakeshore Rd. When you see Bexhill Rd., turn right to reach Rattray Marsh Conservation Area at the end. The marsh is one of the largest remaining wetlands on the west end of Lake Ontario and also one of the biggest green spaces covered in this chapter. Several trails here give access to wooded areas that are excellent for migrant landbirds, as well as access to the marsh itself for marsh birds and other waterbirds. Over the years, rarities like Cinnamon Teal, Little Blue Heron, and Purple Gallinule have been spotted here. In late summer if the water levels are low, the marsh can also attract shorebirds, with both yellowlegs being fairly common alongside other expected species like Solitary, Semipalmated, and Least Sandpipers.

On a good day during migration you can spend an entire morning birding here. If you're feeling ambitious, you can continue for 500 m/yds on foot along the waterfront trail to the east to reach Jack Darling Memorial Park. If not, drive less than a minute east on Lakeshore Rd. to the vehicle entrance to the park. The south and west sides of the park have lots of wooded areas and a good trail network that can be productive for landbirds during migration. This is also a good spot for easily accessing the lake to scan for waterbirds like Red-necked Grebes and scoters.

To the east, as you drive along Lakeshore Rd., you will enter the community of Port Credit. You should check both sides of the mouth of the Credit River. On the west is J.C. Saddington Park, which offers a great view of the lake for waterbirds and, despite its small size, can be productive for migrant songbirds, including sparrows like White-crowned and Lincoln's. On the east side of the river is Port Credit Harbour. This is a great place to see waterbirds and is probably the place in Ontario with the most Great Cormorant records—so look closely at those late-season cormorants!

Farther east on Lakeshore, turn right onto Lakefront Promenade to enter Lakefront Promenade Park. Surrounded by an industrial area, this park is a series of small wooded peninsulas forming several small bays. The habitat here is excellent for winter owls roosting in the conifers, so be sure to check those in season. The many small bays can be good for a variety of ducks and grebes, such as Greater Scaups, Long-tailed Ducks, and Red-necked and Horned Grebes, from fall through spring. In the winter, look through the loafing flocks of gulls for less common species. The wooded areas here aren't generally as productive as others in this chapter for migrant songbirds.

Less than a 10-minute drive east on Lakeshore, just past Dixie Rd., is Marie Curtis Park, which is actually shared by Peel Region and the City of Toronto along Etobicoke Creek. The park gives good access to the lake for scanning, but is also very productive in migration for landbirds. Some nice wooded sections, particularly along the creek and the south end of the park, can hold good flocks of migrant warblers. It's an excellent place to look for sparrows and other species that like shrubby and field habitats in migration too, with records of both Nelson's and LeConte's Sparrows found here during fall migration.

While it is technically in the City of Toronto, one last spot is always worth checking. Go a little farther east on Lakeshore (Lakeshore Rd. becomes Lakeshore Blvd. as you leave Mississauga) and head south on Colonel Samuel Smith Park Dr. (opposite Kipling Ave.) past Humber College. The road ends at the parking lot for Colonel Samuel Smith Park. Here, extensive trails cover the small peninsula and its sheltered bay. The wooded areas (particularly just east of the parking area) are great for migrant landbirds, including an impressive list of at least 34 species of warblers. The small wetland along the creek to the north is worth checking for herons. Black-crowned Night-Herons are almost always present and a Yellow-crowned Night-Heron spent about two months here in the fall of 2014, becoming one of the most-seen birds in Ontario history.

The park offers excellent vantages of the lake and has become known as a great place to observe waterbirds in migration—each year at the end of May, volunteers count hundreds of Whimbrels as they migrate through the area. Watching the lake for pelagic species like jaegers can be productive here in the fall too. And in late fall and early winter, be sure to check the rocks along the shore for Purple Sandpipers. If you're here in April, this park can be one of the best places around the Great Lakes to witness the huge numbers of Red-necked Grebes that stop over. A Western Grebe has been found here on many occasions in recent years.

GETTING THERE
The route described here follows Lakeshore Rd. and then Lakeshore Blvd., beginning in Burlington and ending in western Toronto (Etobicoke). To reach the first (westernmost) site, take Hwy. 403/the Queen Elizabeth Way (QEW) west to exit 105 and go south on Walkers Line to Lakeshore Rd.

ARKENDO PARK TO COLONEL SAMUEL SMITH PARK

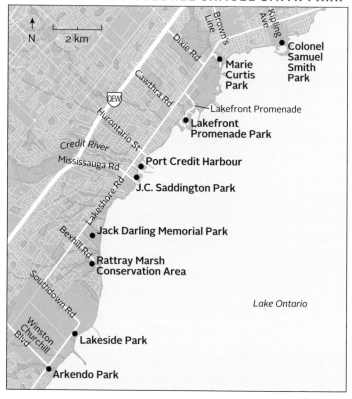

PALETTA LAKEFRONT PARK TO SEDGEWICK FOREST

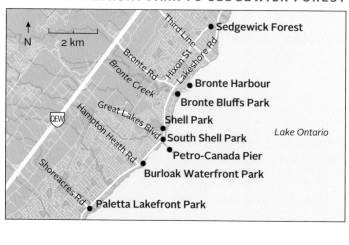

16
TORONTO HARBOUR

OVERVIEW

Toronto, with just under three million residents, is the largest and busiest city in Canada and one of the largest in North America. All that concentration of concrete and people shouldn't scare you away, though—the city is absolutely spoiled when it comes to green spaces and excellent birding opportunities. Not only does the city offer world-class birding, but excellent public transit means it is one of the few places in the country where you don't need a car to get from one location to another. Use the subway, streetcars, buses, or a combination to get between starting points and then explore each spot on foot or by bicycle (don't worry, birding by bicycle won't scare the birds away).

What makes Toronto so good for birding? Well, first, Toronto sits right on the north shore of Lake Ontario, which puts it along a natural corridor for bird migration. Just as at well-known migration hotspots like Point Pelee (Chapter 3) and Long Point (Chapter 11), in the spring Toronto provides a refuge for birds crossing long stretches of open water as they head north, especially when the crossing is made more difficult by poor weather. Similarly, in the fall, birds can "pile up" along the shoreline in natural areas while they await ideal crossing conditions to continue their migration south. Second, while much of the Lake Ontario shoreline has been converted to industrial and commercial use, Toronto Harbour is sheltered by two huge chunks of largely green real estate: the Toronto Islands and Tommy Thompson Park.

The Toronto Islands are easily reached by ferry from downtown Toronto, which makes them very popular with tourists and Torontonians alike as a summer escape. While Billy Bishop Toronto City Airport occupies the western part of the islands, and the Centreville Theme Park and a small residential community cover much of the remainder of the islands, there are still plenty of wooded areas, small ponds, and wetlands, plus kilometres of trails and beaches. The islands attract large numbers of migrants in spring and fall but they also provide great birding on the lake and beaches. The species list for the islands is at least 335, one of the highest totals in the province for such a small area.

Tommy Thompson Park (also known as the Leslie Street Spit and the Outer Harbour East Headland) is a 4.5 km (2.8 mi.) long peninsula built of construction waste and harbour dredgings over the past 70 years. The area has undergone natural succession as well as planned habitat enhancements and is now an amazing green space that's enjoyed by thousands of

Birding the sites around Toronto Harbour provides a magnificent view of the skyline juxtaposed with flocks of wintering ducks and breeding colonies of waterbirds. JEAN IRON

people throughout the year. It's also an important stopover site for a huge number of migrants each year and an important waterbird nesting site, with large colonies of Double-crested Cormorants and Ring-billed Gulls and lesser numbers of Herring Gulls, Black-crowned Night-Herons, Great Egrets, and Common Terns. In addition, waterfowl numbers and variety can be impressive here from fall through spring. The park boasts a bird list of approximately 320 species.

BIRDING STRATEGY

Toronto Harbour offers a huge array of birding opportunities year-round. The best times to visit are during spring and fall migrations and during the winter season. During migration, and depending on the time of year, you'll be able to find good diversity of waterfowl, shorebirds, and landbirds. Winter brings the opportunity to search for a nice selection of waterfowl as well as the possibility of winter raptors, including a decent chance at owls.

Toronto Islands. You can get to the islands by water taxi, but the most economical strategy is to take a ferry from the Jack Layton Ferry Terminal in Harbour Square Park at the south end of Bay St. Three different ferries go to three different parts of the islands and their schedules vary seasonally and by route (check the City of Toronto's website for up-to-date ferry schedules). The western ferry route takes you to Hanlan's Point; the middle route, to Centre Island; and the eastern route, to Ward's Island. Depending on when you're visiting, the ferry schedule may dictate where you can easily go. There are many nooks and crannies on the islands from which to search for birds, so don't hesitate to explore.

Most birders focus on the Hanlan's Point/Gibraltar Point area and/or the Ward's Island area. Centre Island is usually the least productive for birding. If you have a full day or if you've brought your bicycle, consider starting at one end of the islands, working your way through them, and catching the ferry back to downtown from the opposite end. Before you set out, just be sure you've read the ferry schedule properly and don't have to backtrack at the end of the day!

The best time to visit is during landbird migration. Mid-May and late August to late September are peak times for neotropic migrants like warblers, thrushes, vireos, and fly-catchers. At any time of year, however, be sure to check the lake regularly for birds on the water. In the fall, keep an eye to the sky for migrating raptors on north winds.

Starting from the ferry terminal on Ward's Island, wander the narrow streets in the residential area looking for migrant songbirds like flocks of warblers and flycatchers. Continue east (away from downtown Toronto) on any of the numbered streets until they intersect Lakeshore Ave., and then turn left to pick up the path that skirts the shoreline on the east side of Ward's Island. Check the open area here for gulls and grebes, along with other waterbirds, and scan the Eastern Channel between the island and the mainland for waterfowl. In winter, checking any areas on the lake with some icepack can often yield Glaucous and Iceland Gulls.

From the park, continue southwest on narrow Ward's Island following either Cibola Ave. on the harbour side or the boardwalk along the lake side. Particularly on cool mornings it's best to pick the side that's most sheltered from the wind. Ducking across the small bridge to Algonquin Island leads

Migrant warblers, like this American Redstart, can be numerous during migration when they concentrate along the lakeshore at places like Tommy Thompson Park and the Toronto Islands. MICHAEL BURRELL

to more treed residential streets, with forest birds, views of the harbour, and, at the west end, an area with shrubs and a clearing that might turn up sparrows and other birds that like open habitat, like Eastern Kingbirds.

Cross back onto Ward's Island and continue southwest on either of the two parallel routes. As you get to the pier and the Avenue of the Island, you'll know Ward's Island has become Centre Island. It is less densely forested but can still be good for migrant landbirds. If you have been following the boardwalk, you'll now be on Lakeshore Ave. If you have been following Cibola Ave., continue until it merges with Lakeshore Ave. Continue on Lakeshore and follow it to the most southerly tip, Gibraltar Point. The area around the lighthouse can be especially good for landbird migrants: in 1993, Canada's only Variegated Flycatcher was found here and seen by hundreds. As the island curves northward, you can stay on any of the trails and bird the interior lagoons for waterbirds and the wooded areas for landbirds like Red-eyed Vireos and Magnolia Warblers. Hanlan's Point Beach on the west side of the island is clothing optional, so be warned! With people using the beach, however, there aren't usually many shorebirds anyway.

Make your way to the north end of the beach along the edge of the airport. This section is used less by people and offers fairly good shorebird habitat (best from late July to early September). In the spring of 2015 a Wilson's Plover showed up here, as did four Piping Plovers that attempted (unsuccessfully) to nest. Backtrack slightly to the grassy open area just south of the airport, which can be a particularly good spot for sparrows in migration, including LeConte's and Nelson's Sparrows on occasion. When you're ready to return to the mainland, head north along the trails to the Hanlan's Point Ferry Terminal.

For more detailed tips on birding the islands, be sure to check out Norm Murr's *Toronto Islands Birding and Site Guide* posted on the Ontario Field Ornithologists' website.

Tommy Thompson Park. The starting point of the spit is the base of Leslie St. where there is a large parking area. If you're visiting in late fall through early spring, you may want to start by heading west along Unwin Ave. for 800 m/yds to the small bridge over the channel, as this is a great spot to see winter ducks up close. This is the only place in Ontario where we've been so close to a Harlequin Duck that we've heard it vocalizing.

At the time of writing, the spit is still considered an active construction site, so it is closed to the public during working hours on weekdays. There are plans to open the spit to the public every day but no date has been set; check with the Toronto and Region Conservation Authority for current hours. You should also be aware that dogs are not allowed anywhere in the park, so be sure to leave Fido at home.

Depending on the season, you'll want to adjust your strategy slightly. In winter, checking the lake and the various bays is ideal for finding wintering ducks. Checking patches of trees for roosting owls can be productive too, but be sure to keep your distance and stay on the trails. In spring and fall, the area can be excellent for virtually all sorts of birds from shorebirds to sparrows and warblers. During the breeding season, the waterbird colonies are fascinating to observe, with thousands of Ring-billed Gulls and Double-crested Cormorants.

Birding the spit by bicycle is the most efficient strategy, as some of the best spots are up to 5 km (3 mi.) out. And that's just one way. Birding on foot is still great, but you will definitely get a workout! One of the best places to find birds, however, is right at the start: the "wet woods" are the woodlot directly behind (west of) the parking lot. Explore the trails here for what can be the best landbird spot during migration. Be sure to also check the small patch of trees on the east known as "The Bowl," as it can also be an excellent migrant trap. Days with 20+ species of warblers aren't uncommon here.

Start by going south down the paved multi-use "Spine Rd.," keeping an eye on the lake on either side for ducks in late fall through spring. Long-tailed Ducks, Buffleheads, Common Goldeneyes, and Red-breasted Mergansers are the species most likely to be encountered. Sparrows can be abundant in the open areas and forest birds can be found in patches of trees (as can roosting owls in winter occasionally). Eventually the road forks.

Staying to the left will take you down Endikement Rd. along the east side of cells 1, 2, and 3 and to "Pipit Point," a great spot to observe active waterbird migration. Amazingly, a Willow Ptarmigan was seen here in 2017. The small cove ("East Cove") to the west of Pipit Point can be good for ducks, especially during strong north winds, as the cove is sheltered in these conditions. The shrubby areas along the edge of the cells can be good for songbirds, and the cells often hold waterfowl and shorebirds during migration. In 2016 the province's first Common Ringed Plover spent a few days here, and we have fond memories of meeting up at the base of the spit and riding our bikes down to see it. The trail heads west along the south shore of cell 3 and intersects the trail that went right at the fork.

To go out to the lighthouse, go left, which leads you west and then southwest to the point. Alternatively, go right to start working your way back north on the west side of the cells. The harbour side of the spit has a series of peninsulas running perpendicular to the "Spine Rd."—these areas have the largest tree cover and most of the waterbird colonies' nesting areas. The embayments between these small peninsulas are excellent places to look for ducks. The northernmost of these ("Embayment D") has recently been closed by a causeway and is a particularly good spot for dabbling ducks.

The Tommy Thompson Park Bird Research Station operates a migration-monitoring (banding) station on Peninsula D that welcomes visitors when the park is open during the migration season (approximately April 1 to June 9 and August 5 to November 12). It is a great place to see birds up close.

GETTING THERE

The Jack Layton Ferry Terminal, from which boats leave for the Toronto Islands, is south of Queens Quay between Bay and Yonge St. If you're arriving by public transit, get off the subway at Union Station, then walk east to Bay St., head south to Queens Quay, and turn left. It's about a 10-minute walk from Union Station. You can also take the 509 or 510 streetcar south and get off at the Queens Quay/Ferry Docks stop. There is parking at the ferry terminal, but it isn't cheap.

For Tommy Thompson Park, head east on Lakeshore Blvd. from downtown and then go south on Leslie St. to the parking lot. By transit, take the 83 Jones bus south from Donlands subway station to Commissioners St., then walk south for five minutes to the park entrance.

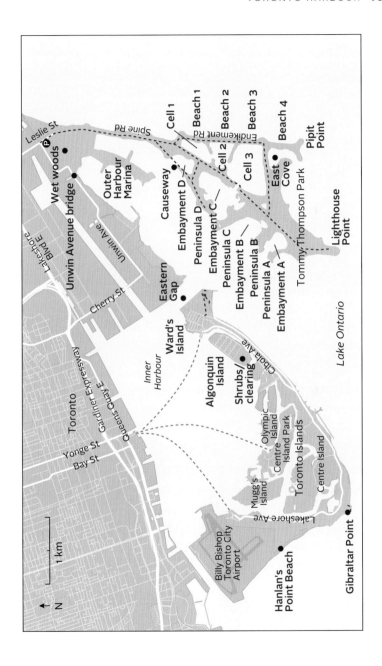

Leslie St

Spine Rd

Cell 1

Beach 1

Beach 2

Beach 3

Beach 4

Pipit Point

Wet woods

Unwin Avenue bridge

Outer Harbour Marina

Causeway

Embayment D

Peninsula D

Embayment C

Cell 2

Cell 3

East Cove

Lighthouse Point

Endikement Rd

Lakeshore Blvd E

Unwin Ave

Cherry St

Eastern Gap

Peninsula C

Embayment B

Peninsula B

Embayment A

Peninsula A

Tommy Thompson Park

Ward's Island

Inner Harbour

Algonquin Island

Shrubs/ clearing

Cibola Ave

Lake Ontario

Toronto

Gardiner Expressway

Queens Quay E

Yonge St

Bay St

Olympic Island

Centre Island Park

Toronto Islands

Centre Island

Mugg's Island

Lakeshore Ave

Billy Bishop Toronto City Airport

Hanlan's Point Beach

Gibraltar Point

Centre Island

1 km

N

A great success story is the return of nesting Piping Plovers after an absence of almost 40 years. Pairs have been present annually on Lakes Ontario and Huron in recent years and hopefully will soon be on Lake Erie. MICHAEL BURRELL

17

DURHAM REGION WATERFRONT, WHITBY/OSHAWA

OVERVIEW

Durham Region sits at the eastern edge of the sprawling Greater Toronto Area (GTA). Not long ago, much of the area was agricultural land, but as Toronto has spread eastward, the farm fields and small woodlots have been replaced by the subdivisions and strip malls of Pickering, Whitby, and Oshawa. Several pockets of natural habitat remain, and these are magnets for birds and other wildlife, especially along the Lake Ontario shoreline.

Lynde Shores Conservation Area includes two coastal wetlands: Lynde Creek Marsh and Cranberry Marsh. For much of the first half of the last century, Cranberry Marsh was periodically drained—first as a cattle pasture and cranberry farm and then later by cottagers. The marsh has been restored for wildlife habitat and for the important natural services it provides, such as water purification. The area is great for marsh birds, fall raptors in migration, and waterbirds on the lake and is excellent for wintering and migrant landbirds.

Thickson's Woods is a small woodlot that escaped harvest and clearing before being purchased by a land developer. In 1983, before the woodlot was developed (but not before some of the old-growth pines were cut), a group of local naturalists purchased the property in an effort to save it for future generations. That group of passionate conservationists has been resoundingly successful, and now thousands of people— many of them birders—enjoy the woods each year. Thickson's Woods and Thickson's Point are known primarily as a migration hotspot for forest birds and boast a list of over 310 species.

Oshawa Second Marsh is the largest wetland in the GTA and together with the adjacent McLaughlin Bay Wildlife Reserve and Darlington Provincial Park forms one of the largest remaining natural areas along the Lake Ontario shoreline. The marsh is a great place for marsh birds and is one of the Little Gull capitals of North America, while the beaches have hosted breeding Piping Plovers in recent years and the woods can be dripping with neotropic migrants in season.

Between these three locations, you can see why making a slight detour off Hwy. 401 is never a bad decision!

BIRDING STRATEGY

There are always excellent birding opportunities to be had at one of the three sites. In breeding season, the most interesting locations are the marshes, which host most of the regular marsh birds of the province. In recent years, the nesting

Piping Plovers at Darlington have also been a big draw for birders. In spring migration, stopping at any of these sites will be productive, though Thickson's Woods is probably the place of choice. Similarly in fall, all sites can be excellent and you should keep an eye to the sky for migrant raptors following the shoreline west. In winter, checking the feeders at Lynde Shores is always productive, and winter owls including Northern Saw-whet, Long-eared, and Short-eared can be found at all of these locations. Checking the lake for winter ducks is another must and regularly turns up King Eiders and Harlequin Ducks.

Lynde Shores Conservation Area. Most birders access the area by taking exit 406 from Hwy. 401 in Whitby and going south on Lake Ridge Rd. At the intersection with Victoria St., go left (east) and then turn south on Halls Rd. (However, you can also travel a bit farther east on Victoria St. to Eastbourne Beach Rd. and park at the larger parking lot. From there, you can walk the extensive trails south to access a different section of the property.) As you drive along Halls Rd., keep watch on either side of the road because the fields here can be full of geese, including rarities like Ross's and Greater White-fronteds. The fields can also be good for winter raptors—during the last two big Great Gray Owl irruptions, several of the huge owls hunted these fields. As you approach the end of the road, two trails lead east towards views of Cranberry Marsh. You can park at either of these spots.

In winter, check the bird-feeding stations at the two access points on the east side of Halls Rd., which can be productive for sparrows and winter blackbirds. Both trails can be good for migrant songbirds in season. During fall migration, a coordinated raptor count takes place daily at the south platform, accessed via the southern trail running east from Halls Rd. The hawk watch overlooks the marsh and regularly gets decent numbers of Broad-winged Hawks and Golden Eagles in season (September and late October, respectively), though the main flight line is often slightly inland. Scanning the lake for loons, grebes, and ducks at the south end of Halls Rd. or from the trail along the south edge of the marsh is always worthwhile too, especially from fall through spring. You will often see good numbers of Common Loons in fall, along with Long-tailed Ducks, Red-breasted Mergansers, Common Goldeneyes, and a few Harlequin Ducks in recent years.

Thickson's Woods. From Lynde Shores, drive 6.5 km (4 mi.) east on Victoria St., passing through some industrial areas, until you reach Thickson Rd. (If you are coming directly from Hwy. 401, take exit 412 and go south on Thickson Rd.) Drive south until you see a parking area in a cul-de-sac just before the end of the road. The woodlot to the east is the famed Thickson's Woods. During spring migration, not a day goes by without several birders searching the trails here. Under the right conditions, the woodlot can be alive with warblers, tanagers, and vireos. In winter the resident Great Horned Owls and Carolina Wrens are both worth searching for, but you may also turn your attention to the waterfront trail to the southwest that goes out to Thickson's Point. The scattered trees along the point are perfect roosting sites for wintering Northern Saw-whet Owls, and at dusk Long-eared and Short-eared Owls are both seen hunting the open area occasionally. From fall through spring, the point is also worth visiting so you can scan the lake for rafts of Long-tailed Ducks and Greater Scaups that may include the odd Harlequin Duck.

From Thickson's Woods you can also walk the Waterfront Trail east, crossing Corbett Creek and walking alongside Corbett Creek Marsh, which can yield marsh birds in season, including Virginia Rails and Marsh Wrens. In 2006, a Garganey was found briefly before it flew farther east to Oshawa Second Marsh. For history buffs, the far side of Corbett Creek Marsh is the former site of Camp X, the secret Allied spy training facility during World War Two.

Oshawa Second Marsh/Darlington Provincial Park complex. From Thickson's Woods, head north to Victoria St. (just before you would cross Hwy. 401) and continue east as Victoria St. becomes Bloor St. After a few kilometres go right (south) on Farewell St. (if you are coming directly from Hwy. 401, take exit 418 and go south on Farewell St.). At Colonel Sam Dr., turn left (east) and follow the road as it bends south. At 2 km (1.2 mi.), you'll pass a large building and a parking lot on your right. Keep going for another 400 m/yds to another large building on your right with parking lots on either side of it. Pull in to the lot just past the building, head to the southwest corner, and park. Here a trail leads down to a viewing tower overlooking Oshawa Second Marsh—this is a prime spot to scope the marsh for ducks during migration.

From April to May, large numbers of Bonaparte's and lesser numbers of Little Gulls will be present first thing in the morning before they head out to the lake to feed. Little Gull numbers peak in late April and range from single digits to high double digits, with some counts over 100! On good days they can even be seen doing display flights out over the marsh. During songbird migration, walking the trail south towards the lake can be very productive, with pockets of warblers as well as forest-interior species like Swainson's Thrush and Ovenbird. The beach here can also be checked for shorebirds and the lake scanned for ducks and other waterbirds, like Horned Grebes and Common Loons.

From the beach, you can walk east past McLaughlin Bay to enter Darlington Provincial Park. You can also access the park by car by heading back to Hwy. 401, going east to exit 425, and then following the signs for the park. There's a small entrance fee for the park that can be paid at the gatehouse. Several small hiking trails lead through forested areas and these, along with the campgrounds, are good places to search for landbirds in migration. In winter, they can also be good places to spot finches, waterfowl, and owls. In particular, the Robinson Creek Trail can be productive for forest birds, as it follows the wooded creek valley. The McLaughlin Bay Trail can also be quite good, as it follows the east shore of McLaughlin Bay. Since 2016, Piping Plovers have nested on the main beach in the park—watch for their nest exclosures (cages over the nests to prevent predation) and the habitat fence around the general area of any nests.

GETTING THERE

This area just east of Toronto is best accessed from Hwy. 401. Take exit 406 and follow Lake Ridge Rd. south to Victoria St. All of the locations in this chapter are east of this point and are accessed from Victoria St.

LYNDE SHORES TO THICKSON'S WOODS

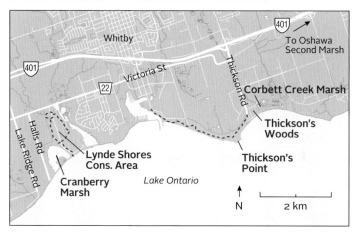

OSHAWA SECOND MARSH/DARLINGTON PROVINCIAL PARK COMPLEX

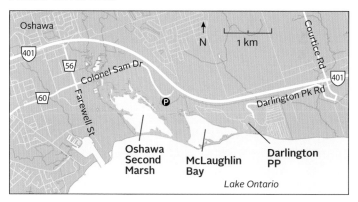

Once found throughout southern Ontario, the Loggerhead Shrike is now in serious trouble and limited to just two core areas: the Carden Alvar and the Napanee Plain. Watch for these birds hunting from atop shrubs like this hawthorn. ARNIE SIMPSON

18

CARDEN ALVAR, KIRKFIELD

OVERVIEW

The Carden Alvar is famous among Ontario birders. Every summer, as spring migration begins to fade, birders flock here to soak in the stunning scenery and the abundance of grassland birds, many of which have declined considerably elsewhere in the province. This area is the transition zone between the granitic Canadian Shield and the limestone-based southern Ontario lowlands—sometimes called the Land Between—and is characterized by a thin layer of soil over limestone, making crop farming nearly impossible. These are tough conditions for many plants: spring brings flooding as the meltwater and rains have nowhere to drain and then summer brings extremely dry conditions as the groundwater lies beneath impenetrable rock. The result is a unique ecological community known as an alvar. Trees and shrubs grow very slowly in this environment and are often stunted, so most areas are open. Unlike cultivated fields of monoculture soybeans or corn, however, the alvar is covered with prairie grasses and an assortment of unique forbs and sedges—perfect for cattle ranching and for a wide array of grassland bird species.

Like the Napanee Plain (Chapter 22), Carden is one of the last strongholds in Canada for the endangered eastern subspecies of Loggerhead Shrike. As a result, it has been designated as an Important Bird and Biodiversity Area (IBA). And at least partly because birders have recognized the significance of the alvar, an incredible amount of work has been done to preserve what is left. Many people and organizations, including the Couchiching Conservancy and the Nature Conservancy of Canada, purchased large chunks of land for conservation, and in 2014, Carden Alvar Provincial Park was established. It's a great conservation story that continues to unfold.

This large area comprises more good spots than we can cover here. Anyone interested in birding the alvar should go to the Ontario Field Ornithologists' website and download a copy of Ron Pittaway's *Carden Alvar Birding Guide*, as it contains more detailed information and many additional sites.

BIRDING STRATEGY

The prime time to visit Carden is during the breeding season (generally late May to early July), but many grassland birds will be present from mid-April to early September or later. Visiting outside of this window will still allow you to take in the alvar habitat, but the specialty birds will not be here.

With breeding birds, activity is always highest right at dawn, although with grassland birds this daily window extends a bit later in the day (compared to forest birds). You should expect bird activity to really slow down on extremely hot days, which aren't uncommon out on the alvar.

A spotting scope is helpful while birding at Carden, especially for scanning distant perches for Loggerhead Shrikes. However, if you only have your binoculars, you'll still see lots. Photography is also very good along this route, as many species seem to take great joy in perching on fences right beside the road.

A good place to start is at the corner of Kirkfield Rd. (County Road 6) and McNamee Rd. in the City of Kawartha Lakes (former Victoria County). Turn onto McNamee Rd. and then make a quick left onto Wylie Rd. This narrow, sometimes rough road is about 9 km (5.6 mi.) long, and virtually the entire length of the road is flanked by alvar on at least one side.

You'll want to drive slowly and stop frequently; however, as you're driving Wylie Rd. and the others mentioned in this chapter (really, any time you're birding!), be aware that you're on a public road and that many people are working or have places they need to be. Make sure to pull well off the road (as long as it's safe to do so) to allow vehicles and, in the case of Wylie Rd., farm machinery to pass. Keep a close eye on the fences and fence posts for sparrows (10 species breed here), bluebirds, and especially Wilson's Snipes. Regularly stop and scan the tops of shrubs for Loggerhead Shrikes. Keep an eye on the bluebird boxes—just before you are 2 km (1.2 mi.) up the road you'll see a small parking area, viewing blind, and bluebird boxes numbered 9 and 10. This is one of the more reliable spots for Loggerhead Shrikes, so scan thoroughly.

Continue along Wylie Rd. About 700 m/yds ahead (north) you'll reach Sedge Wren Marsh. There's a small parking area at the south edge of the marsh, so park here and walk out along the road into the marsh. Dawn and dusk are the best times to listen for marsh birds, including Sedge and Marsh Wrens, American Bittern, Virginia Rail, Sora, and Wilson's Snipe. From late April through May, this is one of the only regular spots where Yellow Rail is detected during migration in southern Ontario—listen for their "stone clicking" calls at dawn and dusk. The shrubby forest on the south edge of the marsh can be a good spot to look for Golden-winged Warbler.

Believe it or not, there is still another 6 km (3.7 mi.) left of Wylie Rd.—keep driving and keep watching for more birds! Some of the open areas ahead are particularly good for Vesper, Clay-colored, and Grasshopper Sparrows. You'll go through a couple of actual patches of forest, which are great for woodland species like Scarlet Tanager, Great Crested Flycatcher, and, if you're lucky, Yellow-throated Vireo.

Wylie Rd. ends at Alvar Rd. (a private drive continues north of this intersection). Make a left to head towards Dalrymple Lake. After 1.3 km (0.8 mi.) you should see signs for North Bear Alvar on the north side of the road. There's a nice walking trail here that goes through some forest on the edge of a great example of an open alvar. Mike once camped here for moth surveys and woke to a Dickcissel overhead. There isn't much here that you shouldn't have already seen on Wylie Rd., but you do get a chance to stretch your legs.

Continue along Alvar Rd. to Lake Dalrymple Rd. and head left (south). Dalrymple Lake is worth scanning for loons or ducks, especially if you're here during migration, but you'll likely want to just keep heading south. Just before you reach Kirkfield Rd. is a small parking lot on the left with signs for Prairie Smoke Alvar. You can park here and walk the track through the agricultural field and forest ahead to come out into some pretty nice examples of alvar. They aren't as open as those on Wylie Rd., so there are fewer grassland birds, but you'll see more forest and edge species like Eastern Towhee and Field Sparrow. You can also access this spot on foot, and since it is less visited than other sites, some people prefer this location over the others.

Once you've had enough of the alvar, head back to Lake Dalrymple Rd. and then turn east (left) onto Kirkfield Rd. This road is significantly busier than those you were birding on earlier, so be careful when slowing down or stopping to bird. Several large alvars and fields along the road often have Sandhill Crane and the usual set of grassland birds. At 5.4 km (3.4 mi.) from Lake Dalrymple Rd., look for signs for Cameron Ranch and pull in to the parking lot on the north side of the road. This is one of the best places to scan for Loggerhead Shrike, and we frequently stop here en route to other places just because we often get to see Sandhill Cranes, Loggerhead Shrikes, and occasionally Upland Sandpipers—all from a quick stop in the parking lot. There's also a small walking trail here that will take you through some great examples of alvar habitat.

With that, you've done pretty much a complete circle—the intersection of McNamee and Wylie Rds. is just ahead. If you've still got time, lots of other back roads also provide marvellous examples of alvar and some very nice wetlands that are all worth exploring.

GETTING THERE

Getting to Carden Alvar is pretty straightforward for those coming from the Toronto area—it's about two hours, depending on traffic, of course. From Hwy. 401, take exit 359 to head north on Hwy. 400. In Barrie, merge onto Hwy. 11 to go north towards Orillia. If you're coming up the night before, Orillia is a logical place to stop and has lots of options for accommodation. From Orillia, take Hwy. 12 east to County Road (CR) 46 and turn left. CR 46 turns into CR 6 (Kirkfield Rd.) when you leave Simcoe County and enter the City of Kawartha Lakes. Keep on Kirkfield Rd. until you reach McNamee Rd. and the start of Wylie Rd.

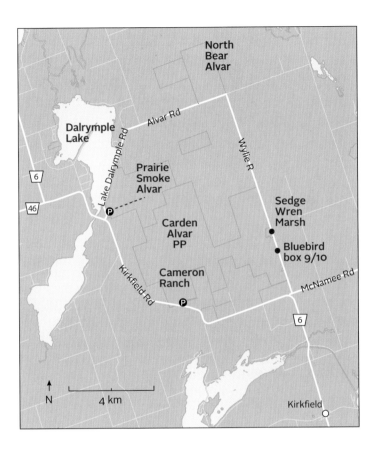

Initiating breeding long before most other songbirds do at the end of winter, the Canada Jay is one of Algonquin's specialties. Try the Spruce Bog Boardwalk to catch up with this species. BRETT FORSYTH

19

ALGONQUIN PROVINCIAL PARK

OVERVIEW

Algonquin Provincial Park is the symbol of wilderness to most Ontarians, and every year about a million people visit the more than 7,000 km² (4,350 mi.²) of park. It's an area bigger than the state of Delaware! Centred on the Algonquin Dome, an ancient mountain of the Canadian Shield, the park came into existence in 1893 to preserve the headwaters of several rivers and act as a wildlife sanctuary. Today, the park is famous for its thousands of lakes and streams, canoeing, fall colours, and Moose, bears, and wolves. The elevation created by the Algonquin Dome results in a cooler climate than the surrounding areas; as a result, the park has small numbers of some species such as Canada Jay, Black-backed Woodpecker,

Boreal Chickadee, and Spruce Grouse—the "Algonquin specialties"—that aren't generally found this far south anywhere else in the province.

Many Ontario birders can fondly recall memories of their encounters with one of these specialty species. We remember our first trip to Algonquin, when we were 9 and 11, and seeing our lifer (first) Spruce Grouse. On another visit as kids, we were on a family canoe trip into the interior of the park. We had never seen (or heard) a Boreal Chickadee but were on high alert. An often-told story in our family is that one morning on that trip Ken shot up out of a deep sleep and yelled "Boreal Chickadee!" Sure enough, one of these birds was calling just outside the tent.

What makes Algonquin such a great birding destination, beyond its size, is its geographic location in central Ontario. Here the boreal forest overlaps with the mixedwoods of southern Ontario, which results in an incredible diversity of breeding forest birds in the park. Species like Scarlet Tanager, Wood Thrush, and Indigo Bunting are near the northern edge of their range here, while the Algonquin specialties reach their southern range limits in Ontario at this same place. A good day can easily net 75+ species of breeding birds, including 20 species of warblers.

Algonquin is perhaps equally famous among birders for winter finches. Their numbers vary widely from year to year, as populations of finches wander across the continent in search of food crops. Each fall, former Algonquin Park naturalist Ron Pittaway compiles information on finch food sources across the continent and produces a winter finch forecast, which has a special emphasis on Algonquin. Checking the finch forecast, eBird, and park birding reports will let you know whether it's a good winter or not for finches. When it is, the park can be amazing: you might see crossbills breeding in the middle of winter and other finches swirling in flocks taking advantage of abundant food. In these years, the Christmas Bird Count could tally several finch species into the thousands. When finches are scarce, a trip to Algonquin in the winter can be the quietest birding you will ever do.

Anyone interested in birds in Algonquin Park should pick up a bird checklist and even the book *Birds of Algonquin Park* by Ron Tozer. Both are fantastic resources that will give you more details than we can cover here. Both publications are available at the Visitor Centre (VC), located at km 43.

BIRDING STRATEGY

Much of Algonquin is not accessible by car, so we'll focus on the main area that is: the Hwy. 60 corridor. From west to east, beginning at the west gate, the highway has markers every kilometre, which makes navigating easy. With 15 self-guided walking trails ranging from 1 to 10 km (0.6 to 6 mi.), there are many spots for a keen birder to explore. All of the trails have something to offer.

Our first stop is a personal favourite, but it's often overlooked by birders: the Western Uplands Backpacking Trail (km 3). Do not attempt the trail as a day hike—it is 32 to 88 km (20 to 55 mi.) long! Instead, bird the parking lot, the picnic area, and the first 500 m/yds of the trail. Black-backed Woodpecker regularly breeds here (including right in the parking lot some years), as does Boreal Chickadee. This is also a great place to check for songbirds in spring and fall migrations. Be sure to do lots of pishing for chickadees. The Boreals are often shyer than their black-capped cousins, so if a flock of chickadees does come in, watch the birds on the edge of the flock and listen for the distinctive nasal calls to locate any Boreals. If you find yourself in the park in April at night, this is an excellent spot to listen for the Northern Saw-whet Owl.

Perhaps our favourite and most reliable spot to get the Algonquin specialties "grand slam"—a sighting of all four species—is the old railway bed at the north end of the Mizzy Lake Trail (km 15.4). You can walk the 10.8 km (6.7 mi.) trail to get here, or you can take a shortcut: continue north up Arowhon Rd. (closed in winter) past the Mizzy Lake Trail parking lot for just under 5 km (3 mi.), where you come to a four-way intersection with the old railway bed. Turn right (east) onto the railway bed for about 500 m/yds until you come to a gate. Park your vehicle, being sure not to block the gate or the road. The 3 km (1.9 mi.) stretch from here on, particularly the area around Wolf Howl Pond, can be great for all of the Algonquin specialties, with Spruce Grouse often displaying to birders right on the trail in April. The wetlands here are also a great place to see Moose and beavers.

Continue east on the highway to get to one of Algonquin's most famous birding sites: the old airfield. The site might not seem too exciting if you just came from southern Ontario, which is predominantly cleared; however, in Algonquin this is a very rare habitat. As a result, some amazing vagrants, including Say's Phoebe, Smith's Longspur, and Long-tailed Jaeger, have been found here. As a testament to the airfield's draw, Mike can recall (with fondness) being assessed on his ability to lead guided bird hikes here when he was a park

The scenery in Algonquin Park can be breathtaking—like this view from the Visitor Centre viewing deck. MICHAEL BURRELL

naturalist. On one outing the hike was interrupted by a flock of Black-bellied Plovers and on another by four Caspian Terns flying over. Both birds are very rare in the park, so naturally, as Mike had just scored a "park" bird for his boss, he was given a glowing review! The airfield is accessed through Mew Lake Campground (km 30.6). In winter, birding the campground itself is worthwhile as campers often have feeders (aside from birds, they may also attract American Martens). Walking the perimeter of the airfield can sometimes yield finches, Canada Jays, and Boreal Chickadees and, in migration, can be good for songbirds. In late September and early October, it's worth walking through the grassy area near the east end to look for LeConte's Sparrows.

If you're in a rush and can make only one quick stop, the Spruce Bog Boardwalk (km 42.5) is probably for you. The trail is 1.5 km (0.9 mi.), and if you're lucky it could net you an Algonquin grand slam. In winter, a suet feeder near the trail register box often has Boreal Chickadees, and Canada Jays may greet you in the parking lot for a handout. Probably more birders have spotted their lifer Spruce Grouse along this trail than anywhere else in the world, and we count ourselves in this group. The best area for Spruce Grouse tends to be around the trail register box (about 100 m/yds in).

Just east of Spruce Bog Boardwalk is the driveway for the vc (km 43). The driveway can be a good place for finches (when they're around) and Ruffed Grouse. Once Black Bears have gone to sleep for the winter, feeders at the vc are stocked and are a great place to study finches at length. Even in poor years, there will be some birds at the vc (some winters this might be the only place you can see any finches), so it's worth stopping here in winter for birds and for the spectacular view of the Sunday Creek Bog afforded by the lookout. The vc also boasts an excellent natural history museum and bookstore. It's best to confirm the hours on the Friends of Algonquin Park website, but the vc is open 9 a.m. to 7 p.m. daily from June to October and then adopts winter hours. Between November and May, it is open from 9 a.m. to 5 p.m. daily (including holidays) with limited services but with access to the exhibits, deck/feeders, and coffee/snacks.

A few kilometres past the vc is Opeongo Rd. (km 46.3), which runs 6 km (3.7 mi.) to the Opeongo Lake access point, where you can buy permits, rent canoes, and scan the park's largest lake. This is the best place in the park to see Ring-billed Gulls (we know, you can't believe we withheld this information to this point in the book!) and in migration can yield other waterbirds. Stretches of Black Spruce along the road can be productive for Algonquin specialties, particularly the area around the gate about halfway north. The road is usually plowed in winter as far as this gate, and Canada Jays are often there to greet you as soon as you exit your vehicle.

GETTING THERE

Algonquin Provincial Park is easy to get to by car: in good conditions from Toronto it will take you 2.5 hours to get to the west gate on Hwy. 60, or about 3 hours to get to the east gate on Hwy. 60, if you travel from Ottawa. During summer, traffic on Friday afternoons can be absolutely terrible as thousands of people head north to cottage country for the weekend. In the winter, pay close attention to the weather because snow squalls are frequent.

From Toronto, take Hwy. 401, watching for signs for Algonquin Park and Hwy. 400, to exit 359 and head north. As you go through Barrie, merge onto Hwy. 11, which meets Hwy. 60 at Huntsville. Continue east on Hwy. 60 until you reach the west gate, which is km 0. From Ottawa, take Hwy. 417 west, where it will become Hwy. 17 (the Trans-Canada Hwy.). After Arnprior, take CR 20 west to the town of Renfrew. Once in Renfrew, turn right (north/west) on Hwy. 60, which will take you all the way to the east gate (km 56).

Remember that a park permit is required when you visit Algonquin. You can purchase permits at either the east or west gate or at the VC.

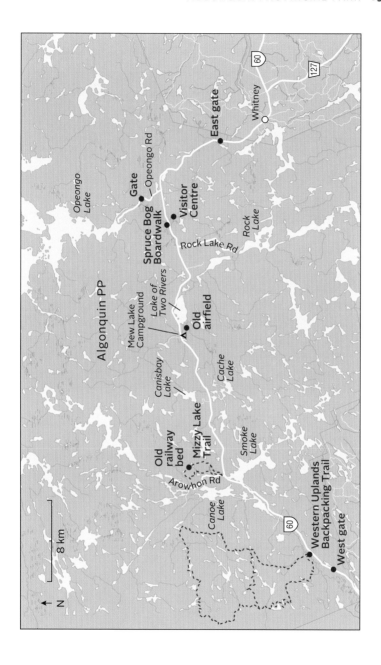

Purple Sandpipers and Presqu'ile are synonymous. These birds tend to show up from mid-November through mid-December. Try Owen Point or Gull Island to see them. BRANDON HOLDEN

20
PRESQU'ILE
PROVINCIAL PARK

OVERVIEW

Presqu'ile Provincial Park, situated on a small peninsula along the north-central shore of Lake Ontario, easily ranks right at the top of the best places to bird in Ontario. The peninsula and two offshore islands, Gull and High Bluff, also included in the park, offer excellent birding all year long, with some astounding concentrations of waterbirds and passerines. Some of the rarest species ever to show up in Ontario have been found here, including Ontario's only Thick-billed Kingbird and Lesser Sand-Plover.

Presqu'ile has a long history. As a protected area, it dates back to at least 1871 when the federal government stepped in to try to stop the habitat destruction that was taking place through forest clearing. In 1922, the federal government turned it over to the provincial government, which passed a special act to formally protect this area, and it became

Ontario's fifth provincial park. Much of the land within the park had previously been cleared for agriculture or cottaging, and over the years much of this private land (including the cottages) has been bought by the province and the leases cancelled. Only the leases along the north shore, on Bayshore Rd., were sold to the private cottagers. The lighthouse forest reserve at the toe of the peninsula and the sand dunes, beach, and marsh area along the entrance road have been unsettled Crown land since European settlement in the area.

Within the park, the habitat is surprisingly varied for such a small area; the bay side of the point has a very large and significant marsh, while the base is made up of seasonally flooded "pannes," the depression-like formations between dunes, dominated by cedar and grasses. The west side of the point has popular sandy beaches and the interior has some nice deciduous and mixed forest. And Gull Island together with Owen Point is technically a tombolo, an island attached to the mainland by a sand spit.

Besides rarities, Presqu'ile boasts an impressive abundance of common bird species, with a species list of over 330. The park is designated as a globally significant Important Bird and Biodiversity Area (IBA), as more than 1% of the world's Double-crested Cormorant, Ring-billed Gull, Greater Scaup, Redhead, Red-breasted Merganser, and Bonaparte's Gull all occur regularly. The first two of these species nest here in significant numbers each year, so you're likely to get your fill of both. Caspian Tern, Common Tern, Great Blue Heron, Great Egret, and Black-crowned Night-Heron all nest on the two islands offshore, which are closed to the public most of the year. However, you can see the huge numbers of waterbirds from the mainland with binoculars or a scope, and you will have a steady stream of birds overhead.

Presqu'ile can be a busy park, particularly in the summer when camping and beach-going bring many non-birders here. But the birds more than make a trip worthwhile at any time of year.

BIRDING STRATEGY

Your birding strategy will depend on the time of year and the type of birds you're after. Presqu'ile, like many other birding sites, is perhaps at its very best during spring and fall migrations. The ducks typically begin to return to the area in late February, but the best viewing is usually around the middle of March. Since the late 1970s, the park has hosted a waterfowl-viewing festival that is timed to coincide with this traditional peak (check with the park or the Friends of Presqu'ile Park for exact dates each year). During the festival, you should see lots of ducks (and lots of other birders).

In spring, the largest concentrations of ducks consist of Redheads and Greater Scaups, with many dabbling ducks mixed in and virtually all other possible species of Ontario ducks. Most of the birds will be close to the edge of the ice, which some years is almost out at the lighthouse; in others, it could be at Calf Pasture, or even on the marsh across from the campground office. Find the ice, and you'll find most of the ducks. Be sure to keep a close eye out for Eurasian Wigeon and Barrow's Goldeneye; both are virtually annual here.

While most of the focus will be on the large flocks of ducks in Presqu'ile Bay, don't forget to watch for Barred Owls in the wooded areas of the park and to scan the open lake for scoters and mergansers. Several houses along Bayshore Rd. have well-stocked feeders that make that area worth checking for lingering winter finches or early arriving songbirds. After the frenzy of activity in early spring, the park continues to be excellent. Through April and May, many birders are focused on landbird migration, and Presqu'ile does not disappoint in this regard either. The best areas are usually Owen Point Trail or the area around the lighthouse. Walking Paxton Dr. from the lighthouse up to "the bend" is a favourite strategy of many birders here, as the road is not very busy but offers a good vantage to fairly low forest that can sometimes be teeming with birds. As spring progresses to the second half of May, Presqu'ile really starts to shine, as songbird migration is still in full swing and shorebird migration picks up as well.

Traditionally, Presqu'ile ranks as the best natural shorebird habitat in southern Ontario. For a strong-flying shorebird that tends to "leapfrog" from staging area to staging area, the overland flight from Delaware Bay on the mid-Atlantic Coast to James Bay in northern Ontario is pretty standard, so most tend to fly right over southern Ontario. However, when stormy conditions prevail and the birds are forced to land, you could be forgiven for forgetting you're standing on the shores of an inland lake and not at a seaside estuary! A good strategy for shorebirding is to park at one of the beaches and walk out and scan with your scope; if you don't see any shorebirds, get back in your car and go to the next beach and try again. Eventually you'll reach the Owen Point parking lot. From here it's best to walk the trail that parallels the beach and check each vantage point. Don't forget to keep an eye out for Brant, as late May is prime time for flocks of this goose to pass over Presqu'ile.

From spring through fall, a short detour on your way in or out of the park at the Brighton Constructed Wetland (along Prince Edward St. just east of Harbour St.) can often be very productive for marsh birds. A permit is required to enter the property; contact the town of Brighton for an annual pass for a small fee (35 Alice St.). Even if you don't have a permit, you should be able to hear the odd clucks and whinnies of the Common Gallinule and the buzzy trills of Marsh Wrens from the parking lot with little effort.

Fall migration at Presqu'ile starts with shorebirds as early as the beginning of July, peaking in August and early September with a few stragglers as late as early December. The beaches can be pretty busy with beach-goers in the summer, so the best area is almost always the south end of the swimming beaches to Owen Point. You're best to park at the Owen Point Trail parking lot and then walk the trail along the beach south, checking at each viewing point.

Gull Island can also be a great spot for shorebirds and songbirds, but it is closed from March 10 to September 10 (inclusive) to protect the colonies of waterbirds that nest there. And from the fourth Friday in September through the third Saturday in December, Gull Island, High Bluff Island, Owen Point, and part of the Calf Pasture are closed on Mondays, Wednesdays, Fridays, and Saturdays to allow regulated duck hunting. When Gull Island is open for birders, it's almost always worth visiting the shoreline (or the pond in the middle) to search for shorebirds, ducks, and songbirds. Getting to Gull Island requires wading about 100 m/yds, but conditions vary; prepare for anything from an easy walk in rubber boots to a waist-deep, icy cold crossing. (Many birders use the garbage-bag technique if they don't want to bring waders: put each foot into a heavy-duty garbage bag, tie it above the knee, and then step into your boots or shoes.) Gull Island in late November and early December is probably the most reliable place in the province to see Purple Sandpipers—usually ones and twos, but up to 56 have been seen on a single day.

If you find yourself in Presqu'ile during the breeding season, the birding is generally slower. Walking the Marsh Boardwalk Trail (opposite Owen Point Trail) will get you a whole host of marsh birds, including, if you're very lucky, King Rail and Least Bittern. Most forest birds continue farther inland from Presqu'ile to nest, but some can be found along the Jobes' Woods Trail through the centre of the "foot" of the Presqu'ile peninsula, including Pine Warbler, Great Crested Flycatcher, and Brown Creeper.

It's always a good idea to check in at the bird sightings board (located by the campground office) to share your sightings and to see what others have reported.

GETTING THERE

Getting to Presqu'ile is relatively easy. It is about 1.5–2 hours east of Toronto (or an hour west of Kingston) via Hwy. 401. Take exit 509 south towards the town of Brighton. At the stoplight in Brighton (Main St.), make a right to travel west through downtown. Watch for the signs for the park and turn left (south) after 800 m/yds onto Ontario St. This street will make two 90-degree turns before you get to the park entrance. Be sure to watch the marsh on either side of the causeway just before you get to the park.

Don't forget that because Presqu'ile is a provincial park, there is an entrance fee, which you pay at the park gate. A day pass is good for all other Ontario parks that day, so you may consider continuing on to other nearby parks such as Sandbanks or North Beach in Prince Edward County to the southeast or Darlington to the west.

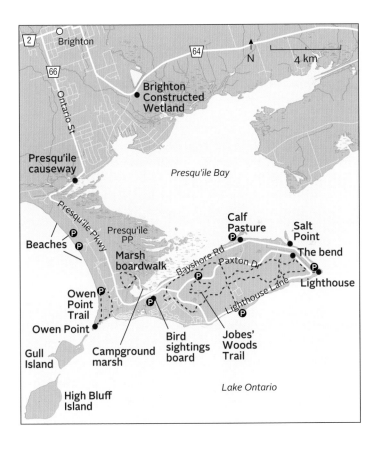

The southern shoreline of Prince Edward County hosts impressive numbers of diving ducks, including White-winged Scoters. BRANDON HOLDEN

21

PRINCE EDWARD COUNTY SOUTH SHORE

OVERVIEW

The entire south shore of Prince Edward County—or simply "the county," as locals call it—is designated as an Important Bird and Biodiversity Area (IBA) for globally significant concentrations of waterbirds, mainly White-winged Scoter, Greater Scaup, and Bonaparte's Gull. The area is also one of the best in the province for concentrations of migrant songbirds. Despite this, being so far from large urban hubs means the county is underbirded, so there are lots of birds out there for you to find!

The county is actually a huge peninsula south of Belleville on the north shore of Lake Ontario. It is separated from the mainland by the Bay of Quinte, and the construction of the

Murray Canal (connecting the Bay of Quinte to Presqu'ile Bay) in the late 1800s as part of the Trent-Severn Waterway effectively turned the county into an island. For most people, the county is still well off the beaten path; it's a few hours from Toronto and Ottawa, and even from Belleville it takes almost an hour to get to the far corners. As a result, the county has mostly remained a rural farming community. In recent decades, there's been a push to take advantage of the moderate climate (a result of being surrounded by Lake Ontario on three sides) and develop several wineries throughout. And retirees have been moving to the area, particularly around the county's hub of Picton, to take advantage of the relatively low cost of real estate and the slow-paced lifestyle.

While large stretches of the county have been cleared for agriculture, several alvars—areas of thin soil over limestone that support a unique open vegetation—exist along the south shore. The provincial and federal governments also own a number of large tracts of land that are covered in natural habitat. Both the alvars and these areas of natural habitat are great places to bird.

BIRDING STRATEGY

In spring, from late March to early May, we recommend heading onto the Waupoos Peninsula. Follow County Road (CR) 8 east from downtown Picton and then turn north up Kaiser Crossroad. About halfway across the peninsula are a couple of fields that flood each spring, the Kaiser Crossroad wetland, attracting numerous waterfowl and some shorebirds too. In late April, thousands of Bonaparte's Gulls congregate here, almost always with a few Little Gulls, often doing display flights right overhead. It's always worth checking along the edge of the flooded field for shorebirds. While Semipalmated Plover and both yellowlegs are probably the most expected species, almost all of the regular shorebird species have been found here along with less common species like Whimbrel and Red Knot. The rest of the year the fields are generally dry and not too productive. Before leaving the area, take a quick peek at Lake Ontario from the south end of the road. The same gulls often roost on the lake and you may also find a good assortment of ducks as well as loons and Horned Grebes.

Head back to CR 8 and go left (west). In the town of Waupoos, turn left (south) onto CR 38 (signs for the marina) to check the marina for a third shot at Little Gull. From there, backtrack to CR 8 and turn left. At the fork with CR 13, turn left down that road and continue through South Bay (you may want to stop at the Black River Cheese Factory too). From here until the end of the road, you'll pass several stretches where the lake is directly to your left. Stopping at any vantage point can be productive for loons, grebes, and diving ducks from September through May. A popular birding detour is to turn right (south) off CR 13 onto Babylon Rd. just past South Bay. Before it rejoins CR 13 farther east, Babylon Rd. passes through some excellent grassland habitat where you can find Eastern Meadowlark or Upland Sandpiper and Clay-colored Sparrow near the intersection with Whattams Rd.

Once you rejoin CR 13, turn right. Follow this road, which becomes Long Point Rd., and you'll eventually see signs indicating you have entered Prince Edward Point National Wildlife Area. Lots of trails wander through the Red Cedar forest, and these can be productive in winter for

Yellow-rumped Warblers and other birds feeding on the cedar berries, like American Robins and Cedar Waxwings. Continue on this road as it becomes gravel, and drive until just before you hit a nearly 90-degree turn to the right. Pull over onto the shoulder and explore the trails on the left side of the road. These trails go through some of the only deciduous forest nearby and can be especially productive for migrant songbirds that favour deciduous forest. You can often spot scoters on the lake from here too. Once you get back to your car, continue another kilometre and you'll see the Prince Edward Point Bird Observatory on your right.

The observatory is open to visitors during banding operations: roughly 6 a.m. to noon daily from mid-April to the end of May and mid-August to the end of October. If you're here during October and can stay until dark, the banding station catches around 500 to 1,000 Northern Saw-whet Owls during this month each year. The trails through the nearby woods can be excellent for viewing migrant songbirds— virtually all of the regular warblers have been seen over the years. This is also a good place to find out what species others have seen recently by checking the sightings board and speaking with the banders. We like to walk the road past the observatory and around the small bay (Long Point Harbour) to the lighthouse at the end—a 1 km (0.6 mi.) walk each way from the gate. Often the forest right at the lighthouse has the most migrants, and a small Cliff Swallow colony is present on the lighthouse itself.

If you can manage it, carry a scope with you because you'll have a great view of the lake from the lighthouse, with a good chance at most of the big water ducks, including all three scoters as well as both Red-throated and Common Loons and grebes. Harlequin Duck and King Eider are semi-regular here. During migration, large numbers of Bonaparte's Gulls can sometimes be seen streaming by—if that's the case, watch for the occasional Little Gull mixed in.

Head back towards South Bay the way you came and turn left (west) onto Hilltop Rd. From at least 2014 to 2018, a Chuck-will's-widow was on territory around the intersection with Brewer's Rd., so it's worth a check if you're here at night between mid-May and early July. You should at least hear some Eastern Whip-poor-wills, as they are particularly common. Keep on Hilltop Rd. and follow the small jog to continue on to Army Reserve Rd. (caution: this gravel road can be very rough, though we have never had serious problems in our small cars). From here to the west end of the road, about seven roads go south and dead-end at the lake. Each of these roads can be productive (keep an ear out for the buzzy trill of the Clay-colored Sparrow) but they can be in even rougher shape than Army Reserve Rd., so use common sense and be prepared to turn around.

Our favourite of these roads is Charwell Point Rd. Again, this can be a rough road with flooded sections, so be careful. The road ends at Charwell Point, which is a small peninsula with a wetland in the middle of it. The wetland can have herons, ducks, and shorebirds, and the forested parts of the point are great for migrant songbirds. In September 2013, Mike came here for some quiet birding and relaxation and found a Northern Gannet flying just offshore—so be sure to scan the lake, as anything can show up, and has!

At the west end of Army Reserve Rd. is Point Petre Rd.; if

you park at the intersection of these two roads, there's a beautiful deciduous forest directly ahead. This island of habitat (in the sea of Red Cedar) seems to attract an especially good mix of migrant songbirds, especially in spring. Look for birds like Nashville and Yellow-rumped Warblers, which are common in early May, while species like Bay-breasted and Blackpoll Warblers are regular later in the month. The whole area along the lake from here to Point Petre to the south is riddled with vehicle tracks that make birding easy on foot. The area west of the road can be very good in spring and fall migrations for sparrows and warblers, while the area on the east side of the road is a large open field and transmitter site owned by the Department of National Defence—this field has breeding Upland Sandpipers and Grasshopper Sparrows (and other grassland birds). You can park at the very south end of the road across from the lighthouse and walk the final 50 m/yds to view the lake. The rocky shelves here (and to the west) are a good place to search for Purple Sandpiper in late fall and early winter, and this is a good spot from which to scan the lake for big-water birds, like scoters and loons, and other waterbirds such as jaegers and gulls.

If you've still got time, head back north on Point Petre Rd. (which turns into CR 24) and then turn left (west) onto Easterbrook Rd. followed by a quick right (north) onto Kings Rd. At the north end of Kings Rd., turn left onto CR 18. On your right is East Lake, an old bay that has been cut off from Lake Ontario by the "baymouth bar" that is part of the Sandbanks Provincial Park beach and dunes. The road turns right at the west end of East Lake and then continues north. The public boat launch, about two-thirds of the way north along the lake, provides a good vantage point to scan East Lake. In late fall this is an excellent place to find Little Gulls and loons.

Sandbanks Provincial Park is to the west, and exploring the beaches here—especially around the "outlet" (where the Outlet River flows into Lake Ontario)—can be productive for shorebirds and gulls (including Little Gulls) during migration. During the summer months, the park is extremely popular with beach-goers, and therefore fewer birds are generally around. The forested shorelines in the park can be very good for migrant songbirds, especially the area around West Point (signed as Lakeshore Lodge in the park). An entrance fee, payable at the gatehouse, is required when the park is in operation, from approximately late April to Thanksgiving. Outside of that time period, you can enter the park for free but many roads and facilities will not be open.

GETTING THERE

You'll want to start your trip in Picton, which is about 40 minutes south of Hwy. 401. The fastest route is to take exit 556 (CR 49) and go south to Picton. If you're coming from the east, you can also take CR 33 west from Kingston to enjoy a scenic drive along the lakeshore followed by a brief (free) ferry crossing from Adolphustown to Glenora, before continuing west to Picton.

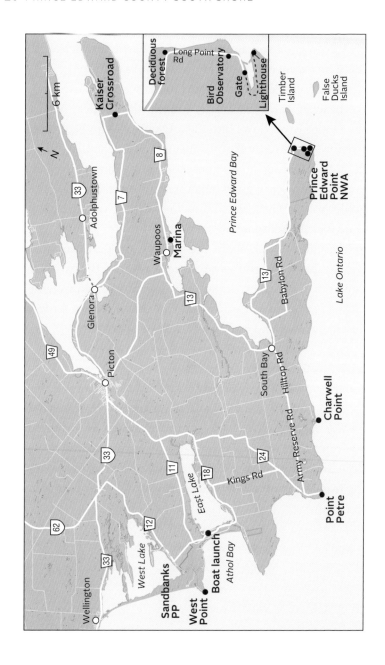

Deciduous forest

Long Point Rd

Bird Observatory

Gate

Lighthouse

Timber Island

False Ducks Island

Kaiser Crossroad

6 km

N

Adolphustown

33

8

7

Prince Edward Bay

Waupoos

Marina

Prince Edward Point NWA

13

Babylon Rd

Lake Ontario

Glenora

13

49

Picton

South Bay

Hilltop Rd

Charwell Point

33

11

18

24

Kings Rd

Army Reserve Rd

East Lake

62

12

Point Petre

33

Wellington

West Lake

Sandbanks PP

West Point

Boat launch

Athol Bay

22

NAPANEE PLAIN AND CANOE LAKE ROAD, NORTH OF KINGSTON

OVERVIEW

In a way, the Napanee Plain and Canoe Lake Rd. areas couldn't be more different, but because they're located close to each other and because the prime time for birders to visit them is similar, we've combined them into a single chapter. These sites are also linked by their proximity to the Frontenac Arch—a ridge of ancient granite that links New York's Adirondack Mountains to the Canadian Shield—and by being Important Bird and Biodiversity Areas (IBAs), so designated for their significant concentrations of at-risk birds. That, however, is about where the similarities end.

The Napanee Plain is a relatively large area that comprises scattered alvars of varying size. These areas of thin soil over a limestone base are managed for agriculture but make for poor crop-growing conditions. Instead, they are mostly used to graze livestock, and those that have been abandoned completely may have a few stunted trees. These alvars support a significant population of Loggerhead Shrikes—about half the population of the eastern subspecies in Canada nests here—and has therefore earned IBA designation. While many birders visit Carden Alvar (Chapter 18) for this species, Napanee is just as reliable. In addition to Loggerhead Shrikes, virtually all of the other grassland species associated with alvars in Ontario can also be found here fairly easily, including Upland Sandpipers, Grasshopper and Clay-colored Sparrows, Bobolinks, and Eastern Meadowlarks.

Canoe Lake Rd.—and, more generally, the Frontenac Arch—was similarly largely cleared by European settlers for agriculture but due to the rugged nature of the rocky Canadian Shield has mostly been abandoned for farming for 50 or more years. In this area, the land has returned to forest cover, and the southern influence of the Frontenac Arch means it is some of the richest deciduous forest in Canada. Although it is slightly less biologically diverse than the Carolinian Zone in southwestern Ontario, the forest cover here is not as fragmented and therefore provides more forest-interior habitat. Canoe Lake Rd. is part of the much larger Frontenac Forests IBA, which is designated for its huge concentration of several hundred pairs of Cerulean Warblers—approximately half of the Canadian population and probably one of the largest concentrations in the world. Many other "southern" forest birds are relatively easy to find here, including Red-shouldered Hawk, Yellow-throated Vireo, and Yellow-billed Cuckoo,

One of our absolute favourites, the Cerulean Warbler spends most of its time high up in the treetops—don't expect to see it this well unless you're very lucky.
BRANDON HOLDEN

while Louisiana Waterthrush and Golden-winged Warbler are both present, albeit in smaller numbers.

We consider Napanee Plain to be the Carden Alvar of eastern Ontario, and Canoe Lake Rd. the Backus Woods (Chapter 11) of eastern Ontario. Though much less well known than their more famous counterparts in the province, these two sites offer excellent opportunities to see Loggerhead Shrikes and Cerulean Warblers.

BIRDING STRATEGY

Birding these areas is best in breeding season, as this is the only time of year that all of the specialty birds are present. Winter is fairly slow but can be good for Barred Owl, especially on Canoe Lake Rd., and the Napanee area in particular has had Great Gray and Northern Hawk Owls in irruption years. Since there are no obvious geographic features to concentrate migrants, it's generally a slower place to look for migrants at any time of year.

The best strategy is to devote a whole morning to the area and to start with Canoe Lake Rd. because many of the forest birds will be easier to detect by song while they're most active, in the first couple of hours in the day. Particularly for the Canoe Lake Rd. leg, you'll want to familiarize yourself with the vocalizations of your targets.

Canoe Lake Road. Perhaps no other road in the province is such a good example of what the Frontenac Arch has to offer: rocky outcrops and rich deciduous forest speckled with small wetlands and lakes. Stopping pretty much anywhere in summer will leave you overwhelmed by birdsong. The Kingston Field Naturalists do an annual spring bird roundup of the whole Kingston area, and we usually start here, aiming to arrive before first light to drive the road and stop periodically to listen. That approach can usually net us all of our target species in under an hour, but we obviously recommend taking a bit more time to enjoy the birds and the scenery!

If you're feeling adventurous, a pre-dawn trip along Canoe Lake Rd. can also be rewarding. We do a Nocturnal Owl Survey route along the road each April, stopping about every 1.5 km (0.9 mi.), and we regularly average an owl per stop, which makes our route one of the best in the province for total number of owls (mostly Barred but a few Northern Sawwhets too). There is also a healthy Eastern Whip-poor-will population. Focusing on rocky outcrop areas and listening just after dark from May through August should net you several of these birds, along with a few American Woodcocks.

The peak time to visit Canoe Lake Rd., however, is from late May to the end of June. Many species will be back by the second week of May, but you're best to wait another week or two to ensure the full suite of birds has returned. Starting from the south end of the road, your best strategy is to drive slowly, stop periodically, and walk small stretches of the road. Keep an eye to the sky for Red-shouldered Hawks, which are plentiful all along. Birds like Scarlet Tanagers, Yellow-throated Vireos, and Eastern Wood-Pewees should be in pretty well constant song along the entire stretch. You may encounter Yellow-billed Cuckoos along the whole road, but they are easiest to find at some of the small clearings around the few houses that remain. Similarly, Golden-winged Warblers are most likely to be found at the shrubby semi-open areas you periodically encounter—the north end of Canoe

Lake is particularly good for them. For Cerulean Warblers, stop and listen at all of the most mature stretches of deciduous forest. The best area is the straight stretch of road north of James Wilson Rd. (about 8 km/5 mi. from the start of the road). They can be very hard to actually see, so locating them by ear is absolutely essential—listen for their buzzy *zee-zee-zee-zidl-zee*. There's usually a pair of Louisiana Waterthrush at the small creek by Rose Lane (address number 10201, or about 12.5 km/7.8 mi. from the start of the road); listen for their rich, robin-like song and keep in mind that this species arrives in late April and can become difficult to find even by mid-May.

Napanee Plain. After spending the first couple of hours of the day in the rich forests along Canoe Lake Rd., retrace your steps along County Road (CR) 38 to Hwy. 401 and head for the Napanee Plain. The open fields with only scattered trees are a stark difference from the lush forests you just left, and the area can get surprisingly hot as there is little shade. The heat doesn't have too much impact on bird activity, though you'll find birds most active first thing in the morning.

Like Canoe Lake Rd., the peak time to visit is from late May through June, but many species of grassland birds arrive in mid-April, so your window is slightly larger.

Quite a number of scattered alvars and grasslands make up the Napanee Plain and all can yield interesting birds. The "Newburgh Alvar," located a kilometre south of the town of Newburgh on Main St. (which turns into Newburgh Rd.), is one of the nicer examples of this unique habitat in the area. It's also a great place for several of the open-country birds you will be after, including Clay-colored and Grasshopper Sparrows; listen for the latter's high-pitched song and scan for both species at the tops of small shrubs or along the fences. This is also a good place, mainly at dusk, for Common Nighthawks, though they can occasionally be found roosting on fence posts too.

The most productive birding route, though, is to head north from the town of Newburgh and bird along Nugent Rd. (a right turn about 4 km/2.5 mi. north of the Newburgh intersection). Just before you get to Nugent Rd., you'll see alvar on both sides of the road. The property on the right (east) is the Napanee Plain Alvar Nature Reserve, owned by the Nature Conservancy of Canada. It is a release site for captive-bred Loggerhead Shrikes and one of the most reliable places to see shrikes in general. Stop and scan several times along here (and around the corner), paying close attention to small blobs on the tops of shrubs and trees—this is the best way to spot shrikes. Using this strategy and driving the length of Nugent Rd. to its east end should net you a shrike, and if you're keeping an eye out, you should also find Eastern Meadowlarks, Bobolinks, and Upland Sandpipers.

GETTING THERE

Kingston is a good base for both sites, as they're just 30–45 minutes away by car. To get to Kingston, take exits 611–623 south from Hwy. 401. To get to the south end of Canoe Lake Rd. from Kingston, hop on Hwy. 401 going west and take exit 613 or follow Princess St. out of town and head north on Sydenham Rd (CR 9). After almost 16 km (10 mi.), you'll reach a T-junction. Turn left (west) here onto Rutledge Rd. (CR 5) and follow it into the town of Sydenham. Go right (north) on Wheatley St. immediately after Loughborough Public School.

As the road ends, stay right to merge onto George St. and then stay right again as it becomes Bedford Rd. (CR 19). Continue for about 16 km (10 mi.) until you reach the intersection with Desert Lake Rd. CR 19 continues from here as Canoe Lake Rd., which runs 16 km (10 mi.) until it meets Westport Rd.

For birding the Napanee Plain, you'll want to get to the small town of Newburgh, where you are just a few minutes from the places mentioned above. From Kingston or CR 9, take Hwy. 401 west to exit 593 and drive north on CR 4 to the town of Camden East. At the intersection with CR 1, turn left (west) and drive into Newburgh.

CANOE LAKE ROAD

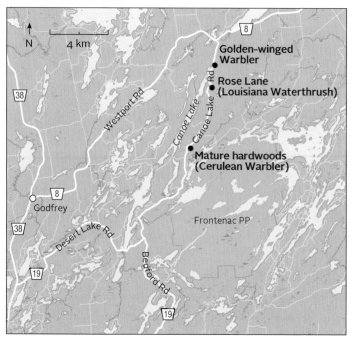

NAPANEE PLAIN

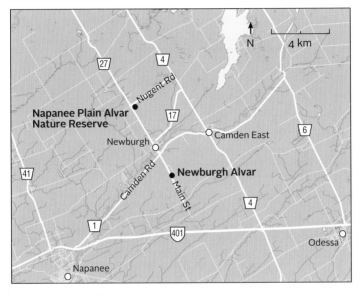

Boreal Owls don't show up in southern Ontario every year, but when they do, they are a crowd favourite —and Amherst Island is the best place to see them.
MICHAEL BURRELL

23
AMHERST ISLAND

OVERVIEW

Amherst Island is a small (70 km²/44 mi.²) limestone island in the archipelago that covers much of the eastern end of Lake Ontario. A trip to Amherst Island feels a bit like going back in time because its famous dry stone walls separate narrow gravel roads and small-scale farms (mostly pasturing of sheep). Besides its stone walls, the island is also famous for wintering owls, which is probably why you're reading this chapter. In years when there's a good owl movement south and the population of small mammals is thriving—and if you're lucky—you could find seven or more species, each with 25+ individuals. Don't expect to do that every year, though!

While the owls can be spectacular, Amherst Island has much more to offer birders than "just" owls because it has an abundance of grassland habitat. Because it's surrounded by

Lake Ontario, the cool lake air delays plant growth in spring and early summer, which means that hay stays longer in the fields before the first harvest, and farmers have enough land to both grow cash crops and leave fields for pasturing. As a result, while grassland birds are declining at staggering rates in many parts of Ontario, Amherst Island has some of the highest densities of these species. A summer drive will yield more Bobolinks and Eastern Meadowlarks than you can shake a stick at, and keeping a close eye on fence posts should also produce Grasshopper Sparrows, Wilson's Snipes, and Upland Sandpipers.

The island is also excellent in spring and fall migrations for just about every other kind of bird, so a visit here at any time of the year will never leave you disappointed.

BIRDING STRATEGY

Birding on Amherst Island can be truly magical, especially during a good owl year. We generally recommend starting at the ferry terminal and driving the circumference of the island clockwise. From the ferry terminal, turn left (east) onto Front Rd. to start your tour. To spot Short-eared and Snowy Owls, try driving and stopping every several hundred metres and scanning fence posts and trees for owls (and Rough-legged Hawks). While they can be active during the day, both Short-eared and Snowy Owls tend to become most active right at dusk.

As you round the east end of the island, Front Rd. becomes Lower 40 Foot Rd. Here, at the southeast corner, you'll find the Kingston Field Naturalists' Martin Edwards Reserve (open to members only), which is often a great place for raptors, especially Snowy Owls. Past the reserve, the road curves around to the south shore, becoming South Shore Rd. and then Long Point Rd. Follow it to the end beside Big Marsh and for views over Long Point Bay and Lake Ontario. Backtrack to Stella 40 Foot Rd. and turn left, then left again onto Third Concession. As you reach the lake, you'll pass the Sand Beach Wetlands Conservation Area. At the intersection with Emerald 40 Foot Rd., go right (north) and then right again (west) onto Second Concession. In winter, Short-eared Owls tend to prefer fields that have some long grasses and weeds left standing in them and there are a couple of good fields like this along this stretch of road, near the middle of the island. If you really want to see a Short-eared Owl in particular, your best bet is to stay on the island until dark. Many days, you'll have to wait until it's just about too dark to see.

Once you've had your fill of driving the roads, you'll want to visit the Owl Woods (except for the three weeks when they are closed to the public during deer-hunting season, from late November to mid-December). Yes, the *Owl* Woods. No trip to Amherst Island is complete without a stop at this small woodlot and plantation partly owned by the local conservation authority and privately by local families. To get there, follow Second Concession to the T-junction and go right (south) on Stella 40 Foot Rd. until you reach South Shore Rd. Turn left (east), drive to Marshall 40 Foot Rd., and go left (north) again to the bend in the road. (Alternatively, you can get there directly from the ferry terminal by turning right onto Marshall 40 Foot Rd. from Front Rd.) Marshall 40 Foot Rd. can be rough and is not plowed in winter, so be ready to walk in close to 1.5 km (1 mi.) if conditions are not favourable. Note that this walk can be fairly challenging in winter.

Visiting the Owl Woods is a privilege, so please follow the rules posted at the entrance: stay on the trails and out of roped- or fenced-off areas and, please, no dogs, no posting sightings on social media, and no audio playback of any kind. Most of the owls tend to be at the far end of the woods (about 800 m/ yds in), in the coniferous plantation, so you may want to walk relatively quickly through the first stretch of deciduous woods (but keep an eye out, as many owls can be here too). Once you reach the cedars, start scanning for roosting owls; many sit close to the trunk and require a keen eye. Farther down the trail, you'll reach the Jack Pine plantation, where most owls tend to be. Northern Saw-whet and Boreal Owls often seem to be on the edges of the plantation or in the scattered trees outside of the main area. When checking for owls, remember to pay attention to the wind: birds will generally be located on the side that is most sheltered (to conserve body heat), so focus your searching accordingly. Long-eared Owls tend to be in groups more in the centre of the plantation. If you're lucky enough to find an owl, keep your distance, lower your voice, and avoid the use of flash photography. If the owl starts to sit upright and compress itself, it is not happy and you should back away. To return to the ferry and your ride home, go north on Marshall 40 Foot to Front Rd. and turn left. The terminal is on your right.

While the island gets most of its birding attention in the winter, local birders know that it's a great place during the rest of the year too. During spring migration, the hedgerows and small woodlots can be teeming with virtually all of the expected species of northbound landbirds. Check the Owl Woods or the Sand Beach Wetlands Conservation Area, which can feel like Point Pelee (Chapter 3) in migration. From the parking area at the Sand Beach Wetlands, walk the trail south. The best area for migrant forest birds is the 800 m/yd stretch through the wooded strip, but be sure to also check the lake a few times. Halfway down the trail is a viewing deck that looks out over the large marsh to the east.

In spring and summer, the Martin Edwards Reserve is the most reliable place in the province to see breeding Wilson's Phalaropes. The reserve is open to members of the Kingston Field Naturalists only, so you'll need to take out a membership if you are planning a stop here. The trail starts at the south end of Lower 40 Foot Rd. (where it intersects with South Shore Rd.) and travels along the south and then east shores. For the first kilometre, you'll have the lake on your right and wonderful grassland on the left. This is the place to look for breeding Wilson's Phalaropes. You'll then come to a constructed pond that can be good for dabbling ducks and shorebirds in spring and fall—Dunlin are particularly regular here. In late September and early October, be sure to spend some time by the cattail marsh at the north end of the pond looking for Nelson's Sparrow. Swamp Sparrow, Marsh Wren, and Common Yellowthroat will also be present and lurking in the cattails. If you continue on another 500 m/yds, you'll come to a couple of big willow trees; these can be excellent "traps" for forest birds in spring and fall migrations. We've seen about a dozen species of warblers in this group of trees alone. Just past the willows is a shallow bay on the left (west/north) that can be great for diving ducks and shorebirds, and the spit/bar continues on farther ahead. If you brought your scope, have a scan for gulls, shorebirds, and ducks—in fall and spring there is usually an impressive scaup/Redhead flock.

Finally, don't forget to keep your binoculars handy on the

ferry ride to and from the island. In winter, Snowy Owls are regularly seen out over the ice (and occasionally a Short-eared Owl is seen too), and in January 2001 an Ivory Gull delighted birders along the open water. During the rest of the year, gulls, Brant, and large numbers of loons can sometimes be seen, so stay alert.

GETTING THERE

Amherst Island is about 30 minutes west of Kingston and about 2.5 hours east of Toronto. Getting to Amherst Island requires a 20-minute ferry ride. The ferry departs Millhaven (on the mainland) every hour on the half hour from 6:30 a.m. to 1:30 a.m., seven days a week, and departs Stella Wharf (on the island) every hour on the hour from 6 a.m. to 1 a.m. The return trip costs $9 per car (motorcycles and bicycles are $2 and $1.50, respectively) as of 2018. You will need cash (exact change not necessary), so be prepared.

To reach the ferry terminal, exit Hwy. 401 at exit 593 (County Road 4). Travel south to Hwy. 33 (Loyalist Parkway) and turn right (west). The ferry terminal is well marked and will be on your left after you cross Millhaven Creek. Service is on a first-come, first-served basis. Arriving 15–20 minutes ahead of the scheduled departure time is usually sufficient, but 30 minutes or more is the safe choice.

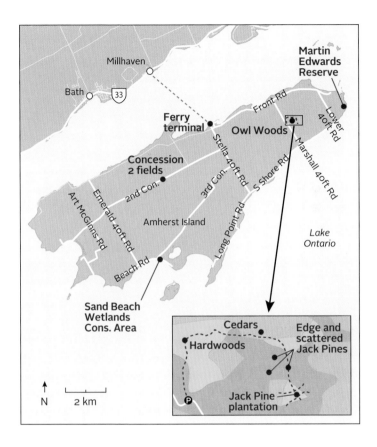

24

WOLFE ISLAND AND KINGSTON

OVERVIEW

Kingston, with its picturesque lakefront, stone buildings, and rich colonial history, is a true birder's paradise. Within half an hour you can be birding the St. Lawrence River, Lake Ontario, Wolfe Island, or Amherst Island (Chapter 23), or head inland and catch grassland birds at the Napanee Plain or the forest birds of the Frontenac Arch (Chapter 22). Mike had the good fortune to meet his wife and spend a couple of years living in this area, so he may be a bit biased, but Kingston will not disappoint—at any time of year.

◄ Wolfe Island has rightfully earned the title of Snowy Owl capital of Ontario, with one-day counts up to 87 individual birds. BRANDON HOLDEN

Kingston is a city of about 125,000. Once the capital of the British colony that would become Canada, the city has a long (for North America) European history. The downtown core is walking distance to the ferry terminal, from which a 20-minute ride past historic Fort Henry whisks you away to the quiet backroads and agricultural fields of Wolfe Island. Both Kingston and Wolfe Island are situated at the eastern end of Lake Ontario where it becomes the St. Lawrence River. This area is also at the edge of the Frontenac Arch, a thin extension of the Canadian Shield that connects to the Adirondacks of upstate New York. The moderating effect of Lake Ontario, coupled with the interface between the Frontenac Arch and the limestone of southern Ontario, makes for many interesting birding opportunities.

Most of the best sites within Kingston are primarily good waterfowl concentration points, but, being on the shore of Lake Ontario, this is also a major migration stopover area for many songbirds. Any lakeshore park is worth searching for migrants in season. Wolfe Island, like Amherst Island, is known for wintering owls (particularly Snowy Owls, but Short-eared Owls too) and hawks, though it also has some great waterfowl spots and landbirding can be excellent during migration.

BIRDING STRATEGY

For birders, the main interest in Kingston will be the waterbirds that can be viewed from shore, roughly from September through May. These include impressive numbers of Greater Scaup and Redhead along with almost every other Ontario duck species. During the breeding season, most of the waterfront hosts only typical breeding species of southern Ontario, like Yellow Warblers and Song Sparrows, along with resident Mallards and Canada Geese. If you're visiting during water-bird season, checking virtually any of the vantage points along the lake and up the Inner Harbour can be worthwhile, and many small parks allow an opportunity to do so. In the fall of 2013, a Thick-billed Murre casually swam almost the entire waterfront of the city, ending up downtown where many birders were able to see it.

Lemoine Point. One of the larger natural areas along the waterfront in the city, Lemoine Point Conservation Area is a great spot for a variety of birds. It can be accessed from the north off Coverdale Dr. or from the south via Front Rd. The southern part of the area is a regenerating old field, which has breeding Bobolinks and Eastern Meadowlarks during the summer, while the rest of the area is a wonderful forest, with species like Eastern Wood-Pewee, Wood Thrush, Pine Warbler, and Brown Thrasher all fairly reliable in summer. In winter, walk the trails through the deciduous forest and be sure to bring seed for chickadees and other winter birds that will hand-feed, and keep an eye out for Barred Owls. Other owls, like Long-eared and Northern Saw-whet (and even Great Gray), are also seen here occasionally in winter. The whole area can be excellent for migrating songbirds in spring and fall—the southern half of the area with younger forest and for-est edge is often the most productive for this purpose and has the added bonus of being a reliable site for breeding Orchard Orioles in the last several years.

Cataraqui Bay. Another must for birders in Kingston is Cat-araqui Bay, which is about halfway between Lemoine Point and downtown along Front Rd. The bay can be viewed from either side of Front Rd. (best to park on one of the side streets as this is a busy road)—you'll likely want to use a spotting scope. Virtually all of the regularly occurring species of ducks can be expected through much of the year. Of particular interest is the small lagoon along the west side of the bay, accessed by turning south onto Sand Bay Lane. Thanks to the warm-water outflow from the plant (formerly DuPont, now Invista), this stretch of the bay stays open in winter and is a great place to pick up lingering ducks, such as Ring-necked, when they are long gone from elsewhere in the province. Because of the abundance of ducks, this is also a good place to watch for Snowy Owls.

On the northeast side of the bay is Marshlands Conservation Area—the actual parking lot is just shy of 600 m/yds east of the railway tracks. Turn up Trailhead Pl. and it's on your right. Marshlands is largely inaccessible but does have a section of the Rideau Trail running along its eastern edge all the way to Bath Rd. to the north. Walking this trail will net you Gray Catbirds and other typical breeding species in summer or White-breasted Nuthatches and other winter forest birds of the area in winter. It can also be dripping with warblers and other migrants in season (April to May and mid-August to October). Part of the trail does cross through some stretches of boardwalk, where rails and Marsh Wren are always possible in season (April to September).

Wolfe Island. Possibly the Snowy Owl capital of the province, Wolfe Island has lots to offer birders. The ferry departs downtown Kingston and, unlike the Amherst Island ferry, is free. The ferry can be quite busy in summer months (a second ferry is to be added in the near future), but most of the year, arriving 20 minutes early should be fine to get you on. Check the Wolfe Island website for ferry schedules. Depending on

the water level, the ferry has two different docks it may use—
the usual one is in the town of Marysville and the other is just
to the east at the north end of "Highway" 7051. Regardless of
where you arrive, you'll probably want to stop at the Wolfe
Island Bakery in Marysville to fuel up before finding birds.
The only public washrooms are on the ferry or at the docks.

Your birding strategy on the island will depend on what
you're after; if you're here in summer or winter, you'll do best
to focus your efforts on open-country birding by slowly driving the roads (the few patches of forest don't have much you
can't find easily elsewhere). From the terminal, our favourite
route is to head west (right) along the north shore (County
Road 96), turn south on 4th Line Rd. (our favourite road on
the island), and then continue roughly tracing the outline of
the island by road in a counter-clockwise fashion. If you're
after Snowy Owls, keep an eye on all suitable perches. Don't
be discouraged if you aren't seeing any at first—often they
really don't become active until the last hour or two of day-
light. While their numbers vary from year to year, invasion
years can be truly impressive; our high is 26, in 2014—a good
tally, but well shy of the record 87 on February 13, 1972. Short-
eared Owls can be more elusive than Snowys as they come
out later in the day. We once spent the entire day on the island
without seeing any, only to miss the ferry. So instead of sitting
at the dock to wait for an hour, we drove around in the dark
and encountered several Short-eared Owls just by the light of
our headlights.

If you're visiting the island outside of winter, there are
great birding opportunities to be had. Driving the roads is
always worthwhile (a Northern Wheatear was found this way
in 2007), but so is checking some of the bays for what can

be large concentrations of waterfowl. In particular, Redhead numbers of 5,000 to 15,000 regularly occur. Reed's Bay and Button Bay are the two most easily accessible bays that often have numbers of waterfowl.

In addition, Big Sandy Bay Management Area at the southwest of the island can be a great spot for many species. To get there, head south on 3rd Line Rd. off Reed's Bay Rd. Big Sandy Bay consists of a trail through young forest and marsh that leads to... you guessed it, a big sandy bay. The bay is popular for swimming in the summer months but outside of that time is very quiet. An entrance fee is payable at the gate when an attendant is on duty, from 9 a.m. to 5 p.m. on weekends from late May to mid-June and then daily until Labour Day. The marsh and forest are both great for a variety of migrant landbirds, and Least Bittern has been seen at the marsh. Adventurous birders can continue walking along the beach (technically a baymouth bar) that separates the old bay from the "new" one. A small viewing platform looks over the now-enclosed old bay. Walk another kilometre and you'll get to the start of Bear Point—the trail continues west another kilometre. We've tried "sea watching" from this point without much success, but if you're up for the hike, it has a lot of potential. The trees along the point here also look promising for migrant songbirds in season.

GETTING THERE

Getting to Kingston is very straightforward from Toronto or Ottawa—from Hwy. 401, take exits 611–623 south and you'll be in Kingston. For the most direct route to the Wolfe Island Ferry Terminal, take the Montreal St. exit (619) and follow this street to downtown, where you turn left onto Princess St.

Follow this road to Ontario St./Hwy. 2, turn left, and the ferry
terminal will be on your right, just past the Tim Hortons.

LEMOINE POINT TO CATARAQUI BAY

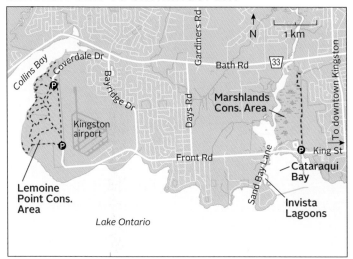

WOLFE ISLAND

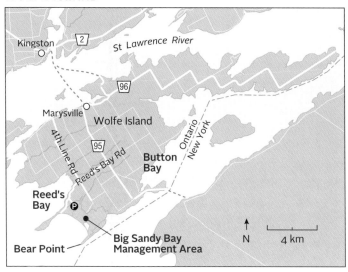

Searching flocks of Common Goldeneye (right) on Lac Deschênes in winter will yield the much rarer Barrow's Goldeneye (left) more frequently than anywhere else in the province. JON RUDDY

25
LAC DESCHÊNES, OTTAWA

OVERVIEW

Being the nation's capital, Ottawa is perhaps the best-known city in the province—at least next to Toronto. Less well known is that the Ottawa River is a major migration corridor, particularly for waterbirds as they travel back and forth between the Arctic Ocean via southern James Bay and the Atlantic Ocean. Along this river are several great spots for birding, including the approximately 45 km (28 mi.) long widening of the Ottawa River above downtown Ottawa known as Lac Deschênes. It's designated as an Important Bird and Biodiversity Area (IBA) because of the large numbers of waterbirds that pass through each year. Most significant are Brant, which can number into the thousands during peak migration (late May), as well as large numbers of scoters, loons, and grebes.

Ottawa is situated at the same latitude as southern Algonquin Park and away from the moderating influence of any of the Great Lakes, so expect real winter weather. The cold and snow seem to surprise lots of visiting birders who come from elsewhere in southern Ontario. As does the traffic. If you're going to be travelling during rush hour, leave extra time (though the volume still doesn't hold a candle to GTA traffic).

BIRDING STRATEGY

Ottawa has a large number of birding sites—there are too many to mention here. Many of the inland sites can be productive all year for woodpeckers, owls, and songbirds, and virtually any place along the Ottawa River can be productive with a scope. The Rideau River also has many excellent spots to search for ducks in season. Winter finches and northern owls and woodpeckers (like Black-backed) can be around some years, so check local bird sightings boards for intel on where they may be.

The most productive sites are generally along the shoreline of Lac Deschênes. The main draw here is the large concentrations of waterbirds, for which you'll want a spotting scope, as the birds can be surprisingly far from shore. The best conditions are during or just after inclement weather in spring and fall migrations, which "grounds" waterbirds that are on their overland flights between James Bay and the Atlantic Ocean. Our most productive day ever here was at the end of May in the midst of several days of off-and-on rain, drizzle, cool temperatures, and persistent heavy cloud cover—we saw flocks of hundreds of Brant on the river and feeding on lawns, all three scoters, a Purple Sandpiper, and Arctic Terns on the lake.

Starting at the west end of Lac Deschênes, one of the best birding sites is Shirleys Bay. This area is the property of the Department of National Defence, and entry requires membership in the Ottawa Field-Naturalists' Club (ofnc.ca) as well as permission from the Range Control Office. Go west on Carling Ave. to Rifle Rd., turn right (north), and park at the north end by the boat launch. Walk back to Shirley Blvd. and follow it west for 300 m/yds to a well-marked trail on the north side of the road. This trail, about 2 km (1.2 mi.) one way, leads through some deciduous forest before emerging on the dyke separating Shirleys Bay from the Ottawa River.

During spring and fall, the shrubby forest along the dyke can be excellent for warblers and other migrant songbirds. Be sure to bring a spotting scope, too, for waterfowl and loons out on the lake or the bay. Depending on the water level, the bay can also be excellent for shorebirds, especially during fall migration, when Baird's and Stilt Sandpipers are both fairly regular. Even on a slow day, a walk here can be very productive. We once led a young birders' trip on this trail during an AGM of the Ontario Field Ornithologists, and despite what felt like a dead day for migration in mid-September, we still found almost 70 species in about three hours. If you're here in winter, duck around the corner from the boat launch to Hilda Rd. and watch for the feeding station. These feeders have been maintained for about 50 years, mostly by volunteers, and can be excellent for winter birds, including redpolls and other finches in good years.

From Shirleys Bay, drive back east on Carling Ave. to Andrew Haydon Park. The main entrance is off Holly Acres Rd., which is virtually at the intersection of Hwys. 416 and 417.

The park is mostly mowed lawns and paved walking trails but can be an excellent spot for birding year-round. Because it's so easy to access, you can drive in and park, grab your binoculars or spotting scope, and scan the beach or the river quickly for grounded shorebirds or waterfowl. Large concentrations of Red-throated Loons, gulls, and terns can also be found here on occasion.

In winter, if there is open water, scan flocks of ducks for Barrow's Goldeneye—a signature species of Lac Deschênes that's easier to find in Ottawa than anywhere else in the province. During migration, walking the trails and focusing on the edges of shrub and forested areas can be productive for sparrows, warblers, and other landbirds—and don't forget to keep checking on the water, because you never know what might have just dropped in!

Another few kilometres farther east is Britannia Conservation Area. You can walk 2.5 km (1.6 mi.) along the TransCanada Trail from Andrew Haydon Park to get there. Or, if you prefer to drive, turn left from the parking lot onto Carling Ave. Go past Britannia Rd. and stay left at the traffic light to get onto Richmond Rd. Take the first left onto Poulin Ave. and follow it to the end, where it bends left onto Howe St. Straight ahead, at Britannia Rd., turn right and drive north to the T-junction with Cassels St. Turn right (east) again and park along the street just before Mud Lake. (If you are coming from the east, turn right onto Britannia St. directly from Carling Ave.)

Britannia Conservation Area (not to be confused with Britannia Park and Beach, which you passed on the way and which is a good spot from which to scope the river for waterbirds) almost always has something to offer birders. In winter, feeders just before the filtration plant attract a nice assortment of birds, including White-breasted Nuthatch and Downy

Woodpecker—many of which will readily take seed directly from your outstretched hand. There are fairly extensive trails encircling Mud Lake, which are also good year-round; if you're lucky, you may come across one of the resident Great Horned Owls. During migration, the area on the north side of Cassels St.—known as the Britannia Ridge—is a real magnet for rarities. In addition to virtually every regular songbird, rarities like White-eyed Vireo and Black-throated Gray Warbler have been found here recently.

At the end of Cassels St. is the Britannia filtration plant. Staying to the north (left), the road dead-ends at the river, and this is another excellent place to scan from late fall through spring for Barrow's Goldeneye in the rapids. It is also a great place to search for rare gulls and jaegers and is probably the single most reliable spot for Arctic Tern in southern Ontario—check for them in late May and early June during miserable weather.

GETTING THERE

Ottawa is hard to miss, but it is a long way from many other parts of the province. It's about a five-hour drive from Toronto via Hwys. 401, 416, and 417, a fact not lost on many southern Ontario birders who grumble (just a little) every time a rare bird is found in Ottawa—which seems to happen a lot! All the Lac Deschênes birding sites are accessed off Carling Ave. If you're driving from Hwy. 401, take exit 721 to merge onto Hwy. 416. Travel this road north to its end in Ottawa and begin to merge onto eastbound Hwy. 417. Just before you merge, take the exit for Holly Acres Rd. and go north to Carling Ave. Head east on Carling for Britannia or west for Shirleys Bay. Andrew Haydon Park is straight ahead.

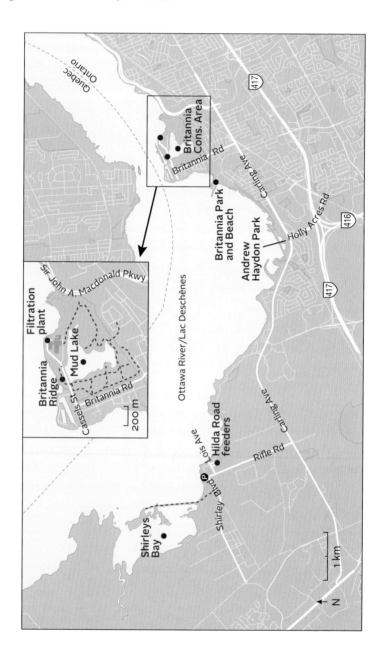

26

LAKE ST. LAWRENCE, MORRISBURG TO CORNWALL

OVERVIEW

Easternmost Ontario, as the area east of Morrisburg is sometimes called, is in many ways forgotten by Ontarians and birders alike. This is a real shame, as some very rare birds have been found here, including Smew, Long-billed Murrelet, and Atlantic Puffin. Over the last decade or so, flocks of tens or even hundreds of thousands of Greater Snow Geese have been stopping over in this area en route from their nesting grounds in the eastern Canadian Arctic to their wintering grounds in the Chesapeake Bay area on the mid-Atlantic seaboard. Though they traditionally touched down farther along the St. Lawrence River in Quebec, they have slowly been shifting west to include this part of Ontario. Seeing these huge flocks in migration should be on every birder's bucket list.

This part of the province was one of the first to be settled by Europeans, with the result that many families have lived in this area longer than Canada has been a country. The area was also a stronghold for United Empire Loyalists, people loyal to the British Crown who were forced to leave the United States after the American Revolution. All this settlement means the forests have been cleared for a very long time, and, more recently, the buildings from several small towns here were moved and their owners relocated before much of the area was flooded by the construction of a hydroelectric dam in Cornwall in 1958. The current water line is not the original level at all.

The dam created Lake St. Lawrence (really it is a stretch of river—you'll see the current when you're close), which reaches from Cornwall almost to the town of Iroquois, but the best birding areas are downstream of Morrisburg. Here there are an impossible number of nooks and crannies for ducks and other waterbirds to hide in, just waiting for you to find them. A large assortment of waterbirds can be found from fall through spring, including an excellent Brant flight. Young deciduous forest lines the lakeshore, but the land away from the water has been cleared for agriculture and supports open-country species. Although this whole area is very under-birded because few birders live here—and the 1.5-hour drive deters some Ottawa birders—it's well worth the visit.

BIRDING STRATEGY
Literally hundreds of small pull-offs, parks, and marinas provide good vantage points along the river. All of them are worth stopping at and having a look, but our favourite spots are those mentioned below.

During spring and fall migrations, virtually the entire Greater Snow Goose population passes along the lower stretches of the St. Lawrence River, numbering into the hundreds of thousands. MICHAEL BURRELL

As a general strategy if you're here looking for flocks of Snow Geese, fall (from late September through early December) tends to be a bit better than spring (variable, depends on ice and snow conditions), particularly because birds stick around for longer and are easier to find. In either season, try to be along the river at first light and look for flocks taking off for agricultural fields farther inland, where the geese spend the day feeding.

Ault Island/Upper Canada Migratory Bird Sanctuary. Just east of Upper Canada Village on Hwy. 2 is Ault Island Rd. Turn south and you'll quickly be on a small causeway headed for Ault Island. The shallow water on either side can have an impressive concentration of ducks, particularly Ring-necked Ducks in spring and fall. Right before it ices up in fall and right after it opens in spring tend to be the best times to see them. At the south end of the causeway, park your car and walk or bicycle in either direction along a gravel pathway that can offer a good assortment of warblers, vireos, and other landbirds in migration and more views of the sheltered water. Heading west on this path will eventually take you over a pedestrian bridge that crosses from the island back to the mainland at Upper Canada Village—a Smew was here in late 2015. Heading east will eventually take you to the Upper Canada Migratory Bird Sanctuary, but it's a long walk; most people walk for a bit and then head back to their car.

To get to the bird sanctuary by car, retrace your route to Hwy. 2 and continue east to the next road (Aultsville Rd.) and signs for the Upper Canada Migratory Bird Sanctuary. Follow the road south, staying left as it becomes Morrisons Rd., to the large parking lot. There is a small visitor centre here and a viewing area from which to look out over a dug pond where banding takes place in late summer and fall (the sanctuary bands about 7,500 waterfowl each year). Several walking trails go through a variety of habitats, including marsh and mixed forest. These areas can be good for migrant waterbirds (especially Hooded Merganser) and landbirds, including sparrows and warblers. Continue south to another causeway (the road is closed to vehicle traffic from October to mid-May), this one leading to Nairne and then Morrison Islands, where the sanctuary's campsites are located. Birding the causeway and the shoreline can be productive for waterbirds in migration seasons and can also be really good for landbird migrants.

Long Sault Parkway. Mike's in-laws live not far from this area, and when he first discovered the Long Sault Pkwy., he couldn't believe he had never heard of this spot before. Just 10 minutes east of Ault Island on Hwy. 2, it has everything a birder could want—easy access to dozens of vantages to big open water and sheltered bays, shrubby forest edge, marshes, beaches . . . the list goes on. The parkway starts just east of Ingleside and travels 10 km (6 mi.) across 10 islands linked by small causeways to rejoin Hwy. 2 just west of Long Sault. Some of the larger islands have beaches, picnic areas, hiking trails, and campgrounds. You could spend a whole day just birding the parkway and it wouldn't be time wasted.

An excellent variety of waterfowl is present from September through May, and it's very likely that if you bird the site routinely during that time Eurasian Wigeon and Barrow's Goldeneye will turn up. Loons and grebes are also frequently observed here, and Snow Geese and large numbers of Canada Geese are also regular visitors. Songbird migration can be very good and just walking along the parkway and birding the edge of the shrubby forests is a simple, yet effective, way to maximize your finds. These will include kinglets, sparrows, warblers, and more, depending on the season. Although we have never done it, birding the parkway by bicycle would be another efficient strategy. The parkway is closed to vehicle traffic in winter. At this time of year (and in spring and fall), driving along Hwy. 2 can be productive, especially Hoople Bay if it's ice free.

Cornwall. Most of the area above the Moses-Saunders Power Dam is part of Guindon Park. This large area is worth exploring on foot if you have time and want to search for migrant warblers, vireos, flycatchers, and other songbirds in season. However, the main point of interest here is in taking every chance you can to search the open water for gulls, ducks, and other waterbirds. In particular, this is a great spot to find scoters and grebes and other big-lake waterbirds. A scope is really a necessity, as this is a big expanse of water. At the west end of Guindon Park is a boat launch area that offers the best vantage point. You can continue east from here searching the woods, but unfortunately the berm (and the vantage over the water it would offer) is now off-limits. In the past, this area was a great magnet for rarities (Ontario's first and only recorded Long-billed Murrelet showed up here), but it no longer attracts the same number of birds it once did, and access to some of the most productive areas around the dam itself is now restricted due to security concerns.

GETTING THERE

If you're coming from the east, then this birding area is the first place you'll encounter in Ontario. All of the sites in this chapter are accessed from Hwy. 2, which parallels the shoreline of the St. Lawrence River (and Hwy. 401). From Toronto, you'll want to take Hwy. 401 east to exit 750 (about four hours) and head south to Hwy. 2 at Morrisburg. From Ottawa, you can take Bank St. south, which will take you right to Morrisburg. From Morrisburg, continue east on Hwy. 2 and you'll reach the area pretty quickly.

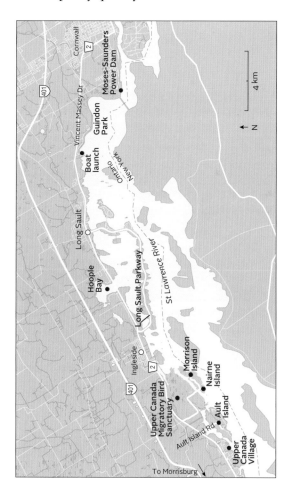

While driving along Hwy. 638, watch for Olive-sided Flycatchers perched at the top of conifers or dead trees next to northern wetlands. MICHAEL BURRELL

27
SAULT STE. MARIE

OVERVIEW

Sault Ste. Marie is the gateway to Lake Superior, which makes its location significant both geographically and ecologically. Situated along the St. Mary's River, which connects Lake Superior and Lake Huron via the North Channel, and just 80 km (50 mi.) north of Lake Michigan, this region is heavily moderated by the three Great Lakes. It is also located in or within 1.5 hours of nearly a third of the ecoregions in Ontario, which means it has a unique mix and high diversity of bird species. Visitors can explore coastal marshes, agricultural fields with hints of prairie elements, rich deciduous forests, and northern bogs. In summer, birders can easily see 100+ species in a day by exploring these diverse habitats.

Although you won't find hordes of birders, like at Point Pelee (Chapter 3) in spring or at Van Wagner's (Chapter 14) on a brisk northeast wind in September, Sault Ste. Marie has a rich history of birders in the area and a number of great rarities have shown up here over the years. Birding in the region can be good at any time of the year; however, given the region's cold and snowy winters, there is much less diversity when the lakes freeze. During migration, especially along the shorelines, it can be excellent and the breeding season can yield around 20 species of warblers in a day. The region is also known for its western affinity, with local breeders including Brewer's Blackbird, Sharp-tailed Grouse, LeConte's Sparrow, Sedge Wren, and occasionally Yellow Rail and Western Meadowlark.

BIRDING STRATEGY

As is the norm in northern Ontario, be prepared to drive a fair bit to cover a large area. We have divided this section into two main areas: Sault Ste. Marie and the Echo Bay–Desbarats area. Depending on the time of year you're here, and how much time you have, you may want to visit these sites in a different order than we've suggested below, or skip some of them altogether.

Sault Ste. Marie. Starting in downtown Sault Ste. Marie, check the Sault Ste. Marie Canal National Historic Site, which comprises the Sault Locks and Whitefish Island. In winter, the river remains open and has, over the years, produced Harlequin Duck with some regularity, as well as lots of other waterfowl. Common Goldeneyes, Common Mergansers, Long-tailed Ducks, and Hooded Mergansers regularly winter here, while during migration the entire river can be good for a number of waterfowl and other waterbirds, such as Common Loons and Horned and Red-necked Grebes. Walking the large number of trails on Whitefish Island in migration can be excellent too and has produced just about all of the warblers, sparrows, flycatchers, and vireos over the years that one would expect in this area of Ontario.

Once we've checked the locks and Whitefish Island, we generally like to drive east on Bay and Queen Sts. to check scattered locations along the river to Bellevue Park. In summer, Barn and Tree Swallows are generally foraging along the shoreline, while Common Terns, Double-crested Cormorants, and the odd Common Loon are on the river. Bellevue Park provides another good vantage of the river, and visitors can expect a similar variety of species as at the Sault Locks.

Echo Bay–Desbarats. From Sault Ste. Marie, you'll have to drive Hwy. 17B for close to 25 km (16 mi.) to reach Echo Bay. Just before you come into the community, you'll drive over a small causeway. Pull off to the side and check the river on your right (west) and Lake George on your left (east). The river can be quite active throughout the year here, with Bald Eagles, Common Terns, and Double-crested Cormorants in summer, while Lake George in summer has breeding Black Terns and Osprey. Continuing south into Echo Bay, take a left on Church St. and another quick left on Lake St. Drive to the north end of the road to check the observation tower that overlooks Lake George. Sora, American Bittern, Marsh Wren, Wilson's Snipe, and Swamp Sparrow are common here in the summer, while scanning the lake in migration can be productive for a variety of dabbling ducks.

As you drive east out of Echo Bay on Church St., keep a keen eye on the agricultural fields; Brewer's Blackbirds are here in summer, particularly in fields with cattle. LeConte's Sparrows and Yellow Rails have also been present in wet years. Continue south on Hwy. 17B until you come to a T-junction with Bar River Rd. Go right (west) and then turn left (south) on Lakeview Rd. for a few kilometres, stopping every so often to look for Sharp-tailed Grouse. Eastern Towhees are present occasionally; this is just about as far north as their range extends in Ontario. The shrubby habitats can be good for a number of old-field species. Continue on Lakeview Rd. until you come to Pumpkin Point Rd. Go right (west) and follow the road for a few kilometres to Pumpkin Point Marsh. The marsh has a small boardwalk and observation tower and is one of the finest coastal marshes in all of the Great Lakes. It is excellent for Sora, Virginia Rail, and American Bittern. Swamp Sparrow and Marsh Wren are also common here, while the ash swamp adjacent to the marsh can have Black-billed Cuckoo and Eastern Wood-Pewee in summer.

From Pumpkin Point, turn around and head east on Pumpkin Point Rd. to Hwy. 17. Turn right, following the highway south and east for about 18 km (11 mi.) to the small village of Desbarats. Start by checking the sewage lagoons on the northeast side of town. To get there, turn left (north) off the highway onto Lake Huron Dr. and then take a right on Johnson Dr. and park at the end of the street. The lagoons generally have high water, but they are a good spot to see a number of waterfowl, including Wood Duck, Blue-winged Teal, and American Black Duck.

Complete your loop to Echo Bay by getting back on Hwy. 17 and continuing east for another 3 km (1.9 mi.) to Gordon Lake Rd. Turn left (north) and drive slowly through this largely agricultural area; scattered throughout are a number of regenerating fields that host species like Clay-colored and LeConte's Sparrows, Sedge Wren, Brewer's Blackbird, and the odd Sharp-tailed Grouse and Golden-winged Warbler. As you continue north towards Hwy. 638, you'll cross onto the Canadian Shield and the farms will fade into forest. The diversity of warblers along this stretch is particularly excellent in June, with Cape May, Canada, Magnolia, and Blackburnian Warblers present, among many others. At this time of year, you can easily spend a whole morning birding the Gordon Lake Rd./Hwy. 638 loop, and it is one of our favourites in the area. In the wet, open conifer stands, listen for the *quick-three-beers* of Olive-sided Flycatchers, and look for Blue-headed Vireo, Canada Jay, and Boreal Chickadee. When driving this road in the winter, pay attention for any finches feeding alongside the road: Evening Grosbeak and both Red and White-winged Crossbills are possible here, while Spruce and particularly Ruffed Grouse can be found.

GETTING THERE

Sault Ste. Marie is a full-service community with an international airport served by daily flights to and from Toronto. If you're driving, the region is easily reached from southern Ontario. It's approximately 4.5 hours from Toronto to Sudbury along Hwys. 400 and 69 and then about 3.5 hours from Sudbury to Sault Ste. Marie along Hwy. 17, for a total of 8 hours. From Ottawa, follow Hwy. 17 west for 9 hours to Sault Ste. Marie. And from Thunder Bay, follow Hwy. 17 east and south for 8 hours.

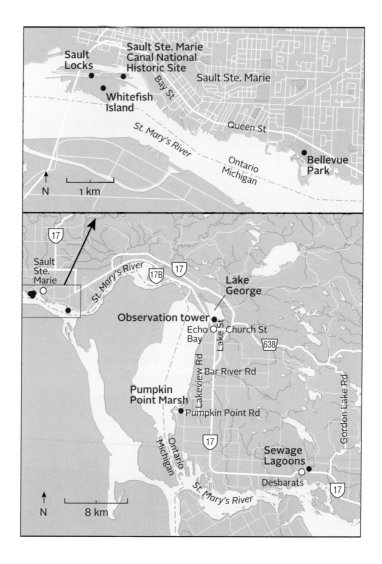

28
MOOSONEE

OVERVIEW

Home to the local Indigenous peoples now known collectively as the Moose Cree First Nation, Moosonee is the gateway to the far north of Ontario. Europeans first visited the region in the 17th century, and nearby Moose Factory is located on the site of the Hudson's Bay Company's second trading post, founded in 1673. Today, Moosonee is a transportation hub, notably, the northern terminus of the Ontario Northland Railway and the southern end of the James Bay Winter Road. Located within the Hudson Bay Lowlands, the region is heavily influenced by its flat topography and subarctic climate, which is moderated by James Bay. It's the farthest south in the province that isolated patches of permafrost exist, and yet wildlife—including seals, Belugas, Woodland Caribou, and birds—is abundant. Known in Cree as Pei lay sheesh kow, "an area that abounds with birds," the region is designated as one of the most significant Important Bird and Biodiversity Areas (IBAS) in the province, for its more than 270 species of birds, at least 15 of which regularly occur in global or continental levels of significance. Among these species, shorebirds and waterbirds dominate.

Getting to Moosonee is half the fun. Most visitors drive to Cochrane and then take the five-hour train ride through expansive and seemingly never-ending stands of stunted Black Spruce. (It is also possible to fly from Cochrane or Timmins to Moosonee, but this approach is very costly.) Every time we visit, we press our faces to the train windows, hoping to catch a glimpse of a flock of Sharp-tailed Grouse exploding off the tracks or a Northern Hawk Owl perched at the top of a tree or utility pole. The tracks end at Moosonee, and Moose Factory is a short water-taxi ride across the Moose River. These communities are the easiest locations to access year-round and offer a variety of habitats and locations to check, including the Moosonee sewage lagoons and landfill, and the waterfronts of both towns. Along the James Bay coastline, the most accessible location is Ship Sands Island, known as the Moose River Migratory Bird Sanctuary, at the mouth of the Moose River. During peak shorebird season (generally July and August), thousands of shorebirds are present on the vast tidal flats.

Remote points along the coast, such as Netitishi, Longridge, and Northbluff Points, are excellent places to witness the migration of tens of thousands of shorebirds and waterfowl, with the odd Gyrfalcon sprinkled in. It's a spectacle you won't see in southern Ontario (or in too many other places in the world). Access, however, is via helicopter or freighter

Moosonee is in the heart of the breeding range for many northern species, including Northern Hawk Owls. Watch for them on the tops of utility poles on your train ride to and from Moosonee. MICHAEL BURRELL

canoe and requires advance permission from the camp owners. Access is best obtained by contacting the Moose Cree First Nation.

Overall, we'd recommend travelling to this area in late summer and fall, as the winters are some of the longest in the province, with snow and ice from mid-November to mid-May. The bugs in the summer can be pretty intense (to put it mildly), though the birding is fantastic and provides a real glimpse into a different world. Once in Moosonee, travel to the coastline can be challenging and expensive, though well worth it. In Moosonee itself, most birding is done on foot.

BIRDING STRATEGY

In general, there are two main areas to check: the towns of Moosonee and Moose Factory and the coastal marshes and beaches.

No birder's visit to Moosonee is complete without a trip to the sewage lagoons! From the train station in Moosonee, take a right (west) onto Atim Rd., which quickly becomes Percy's Way. Follow this road for about 1.5 km (0.9 mi.) to a T-junction. Turn right (southwest) onto Quarry Rd. and continue a further 2.5 km (1.6 mi.). You'll find the lagoons on your right (west). The two cells can be productive for waterfowl, with Lesser Scaup, Bufflehead, and American Black Duck present in good numbers during the warmer months. Along the way, keep an ear out for any songbird flocks. There are often Boreal Chickadees and Canada Jays along this stretch of road, and species like Black-backed and American Three-toed Woodpeckers may also be present.

The landfill is a further kilometre southwest of the lagoons, along Quarry Rd. This spot can be good for gulls, with Glaucous and Great Black-backed Gulls regular in the fall and early spring, not to mention the large flock of Common Ravens.

Heading back to town, it's always worth walking the town of Moosonee itself and scanning both yards and undeveloped lots, as they can be good for lost passerines. A good number of vagrants have been found this way over the years too. Finches and sparrows can be especially plentiful from mid-August through October. The baseball field at the corner of Veteran's Rd. and Ferguson Rd. can have Black-bellied Plovers and other shorebirds, as well as flocks of American Pipits and Lapland Longspurs in season (May and from September to October).

To view the Moosonee waterfront, the elevated Revillon Rd. provides a good vantage point. It's often best to go when the tide is low, as the exposed sandbars within the river can provide good habitat for migrant shorebirds in spring and fall. Ontario's first-ever Ross's Gull spent several days here in May 1983, while species like Little Gull and Arctic Tern are rare but regular in spring and fall. Keep an eye out for Bearded Seals along this stretch too. Heading northeast along Revillon Rd., you'll come to an intersection with Airport Rd. Turn right (northeast) and follow the road to the airport. Keep an ear out for finches—in particular the sharp *chit-chit* calls of the White-winged Crossbill and the warbling *tew-tew* calls of the Pine Grosbeak. Access to the airport is largely restricted; however, the open spaces often attract open-country species and can still be viewed from both the unrestricted areas and adjacent Airport Rd. In migration, flocks of American Pipits, Horned Larks, and Lapland Longspurs are regularly spotted.

Once you've thoroughly checked Moosonee, head to the main dock and take a water taxi to Moose Factory (in winter, you'll take the ice road; in early spring and late fall, a helicopter). Once on the island, walk the perimeter of the town, scanning the neighbourhoods for passerines, while keeping tabs on the river. The eastern side of the island provides the best vantage point for waterbirds. Also be sure to check the sewage lagoons at the north end of 6th St.

Visiting Ship Sands Island at the mouth of the Moose River requires a full day, and even if it could be done in less time we'd recommend spending the entire day out there. To get to the island you'll need to charter a water taxi from the docks in either Moosonee or Moose Factory to take you downstream to the river mouth (around 30 minutes). Be sure to prearrange a pick-up location and time so you don't get stranded in this remote location. Note that the weather is extremely variable at any time of year, so be prepared for the worst: waterproof boots are recommended, and bring your bug spray. On our first trip to Ship Sands Island, our taxi operator asked if we had bug spray. As it was the end of August we thought he was joking, and we didn't bring any—a decision we certainly regretted. The mosquitoes here, even into September, are a particularly fierce saltwater variety.

On the island, take your time walking northeast along the beach ridge. Yellow Rails, as well as Nelson's and LeConte's Sparrows, breed in the sedge meadows. Particularly along the south end of the island, you'll have to cross numerous small creeks that, depending on the tide, can be ankle or waist deep. It's a good idea to check online ahead of your trip to be aware of the timing of tides.

The river mouth around the north end of the island can be productive for waterbirds, with gulls, loons, and waterfowl present in high numbers. Fall—generally September and October—provides thousands of Brant and Snow Geese (not to mention Canada Geese) migrating through the area. The vast tidal flats are a must-see, with thousands of shorebirds congregating here in migration. Semipalmated and White-rumped Sandpipers and Dunlin are the most numerous, all numbering in the tens of thousands. Flocks of Whimbrel and both species of godwit are also seen regularly here. On days of strong north winds, be careful of the water levels, as the island is quite low and in extreme cases the tides can flood large sections of it.

The remote hunting camps located along the James Bay coast are hard to get to, but worth it for the adventurous. Careful planning is required, and you need to contact the Moose Cree First Nation in advance to obtain permission. A favourite camp among birders has been Netitishi Point, 30 km (19 mi.) east of Moosonee at the south end of James Bay. In late autumn, intrepid birders have spotted exciting rarities here, including an unidentified shearwater, Dovekie, Northern Fulmar, and Northern Gannet. Gyrfalcons are regular along the coast in the fall, as are Peregrine Falcons and Snowy Owls. Shorebirds abound, with hundreds of thousands using the coastline. Globally significant concentrations of Hudsonian Godwits and Red Knots are present, while disjunct breeding populations of Marbled Godwits, Wilson's Phalaropes, and Yellow Rails are present from summer through fall.

Winter in this region is long, with a correspondingly low diversity and abundance. However, finches, including Common and Hoary Redpolls, Pine Grosbeaks, and both White-winged and Red Crossbills, are present. Residents such as Boreal Chickadee and both Black-backed and American Three-toed Woodpeckers are also around, albeit generally less conspicuous.

GETTING THERE

To get to Moosonee, take the Polar Bear Express north from Cochrane. This five-hour train service operates year-round, Monday through Friday. Cochrane is a five-hour drive north from North Bay along Hwy. 11. The route is well signed. A winter road from Smooth Rock Falls (55 km/34 mi. northwest of Cochrane) to Moosonee was recently opened; however, at this point in time we don't recommend taking it unless you're fully equipped with a 4×4 high-suspension vehicle and know what you're doing.

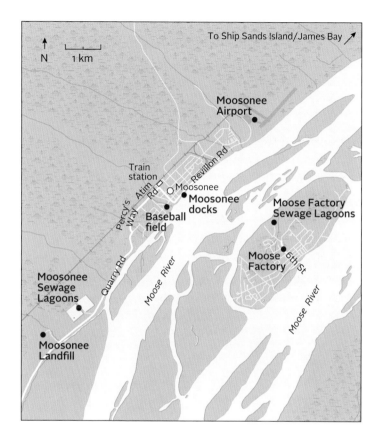

To Ship Sands Island/James Bay

N   1 km

Moosonee
Airport

Revillon Rd

Train
station

Atim Rd

Percy's Way

O Moosonee

Moosonee
docks

Baseball
field

Quarry Rd

Moose Factory
Sewage Lagoons

Moose River

Moose
Factory

6th St

Moosonee
Sewage
Lagoons

Moose River

Moose River

Moosonee
Landfill

29

THUNDER BAY
AND THE SIBLEY
PENINSULA

OVERVIEW

The Thunder Bay area was a major fur-trading post used by the North West Company as early as the late 17th century. While fur trading in the region gradually declined, in the 19th century a major port was established in Thunder Bay to transport grain from western Canada through the Great Lakes and the St. Lawrence Seaway. Today, the port of Thunder Bay is still an important fixture of the local economy. The city is known as the gateway to northwestern Ontario, but more importantly for birders, the area is a hidden gem with a list of

◄ From fall through spring, one or more Gyrfalcons often terrorize pigeons along Thunder Bay's waterfront. Watch for them particularly near the large grain elevators. BRANDON HOLDEN

rare species observed here that ranks with—or above—those at Long Point (Chapter 11) and Point Pelee (Chapter 3).

The Thunder Bay region covers the Lake Nipigon and Pigeon River ecoregions, with extensive tracts of Crown land located literally only minutes from the city centre. The city's waterfront is regularly the only accessible location in the province that has wintering Gyrfalcons, while northern finches and owls can be seen in good numbers by travelling the back roads in late fall through early spring. The waterfront itself is ideally situated along the lakeshore, where significant concentrations of waterbirds and songbirds pass through in migration. But only 22 km (14 mi.) east as the Gyrfalcon flies is the Sibley Peninsula, home to Sleeping Giant Provincial Park, Silver Islet, and the Thunder Cape Bird Observatory (TCBO). Although few birders travel here (their loss!), provincial firsts include Brewer's Sparrow, Black-throated Sparrow, Scott's Oriole, and Violet-green Swallow, not to mention such other rarities as Common Ground-Dove, Sulphur-bellied Flycatcher, Virginia's Warbler, Sprague's Pipit, and Green-tailed Towhee.

Overall, the birding in the Thunder Bay area can be excellent in any season. Winter offers visitors a chance for northern finches (Pine Grosbeak, both species of redpolls and crossbills), Bohemian Waxwing, owls, and the elusive Gyrfalcon, while summer provides a good opportunity to explore the backwoods for boreal and mixedwoods species. Spring and fall migration, like anywhere along the shoreline of the Great Lakes, can be exceptional depending on your timing and the weather conditions. Any green spaces along the lakeshore can be attractive for migrants and checking them can be productive.

BIRDING STRATEGY

There are essentially two main areas to check while birding this area: the Thunder Bay waterfront and the Sibley Peninsula. We usually start at the south end of the city and move north.

At the south end of Thunder Bay, south of the Kaministiquia River along City Rd., lies Chippewa Park, a small point of land that sticks out into Lake Superior. In migration, the open, grassy areas at the main entrance can be productive for some shorebirds and sparrows, while the wooded areas are a good place to spot passerines. In summer, these woods shelter breeding species such as Veery and Yellow-rumped and Chestnut-sided Warblers. Scanning the lake can be worthwhile for waterfowl in spring and fall, with a variety of ducks.

Head north from Chippewa Park along City Rd. for 2.2 km (1.4 mi.). As City Rd. curves sharply to the west (left), turn right and proceed to the dead end, 300 m/yds away. Park here and follow the trail that continues east, leading you to the Chippewa Lagoons, a series of human-made cells along the lakeshore that attract excellent numbers of waterbirds. When walking out to the cells, scan the shrubbery, which can attract migrants. LeConte's Sparrows have bred in the grassy areas, while common species such as Chipping Sparrows and Yellow Warblers are plentiful in summer. The lagoons have had a number of rarer species, including Eared Grebe and Tufted Duck, over the years and are definitely worth scoping.

Leaving the lagoons, head back to City Rd. and go west and then north across the Kaministiquia River on James St. Wind your way through Thunder Bay, going right (east) on Arthur St. and staying with it as it becomes Simpson St., and head northeast. At Pacific Ave., turn right to reach Island Dr., where you go right to cross the bridge to McKellar Island. This island and Mission Island to the south form the delta of the Kaministiquia River; however, they are heavily industrialized and point to Thunder Bay's past as a major port city. Perhaps surprisingly, the islands are the star attraction for birding in the city.

On McKellar Island, turn left (east) off Island Dr. onto Baffin St. to visit the McKellar Island Bird Observatory. It is open in May and early June and from August to the end of October, from 7 a.m. to noon. While a fairly new bird observatory, it is definitely making a name for itself with a number of rarities already (including Ash-throated Flycatcher and Western Tanager) and a good assortment of more common species typical of the area in migration.

Once you've checked out the observatory, continue back to Island Dr. and go south until you reach a T-junction with 106th St. Turn east (left) and drive to the very end of the road, which has become 105th St. Here you'll find the Mission Island Conservation Area, which has a series of trails as well as a parking area and picnic shelter. Clay-colored Sparrows breed in the open areas, while American White Pelicans and a number of waterfowl are found regularly loafing offshore in season. The lakefront shoreline can also be great for shorebirds in the late spring and early fall, while the thickets along the shoreline are attractive for migrants in spring and fall. Many of the city's rarities tend to show up here and it's a great location to spend an hour or two (or more)!

From Mission and McKellar Islands, retrace your route north on Island Dr. and then west (left) on Pacific Ave. When you reach Simpson St., turn right and go north as it becomes first Fort William Rd. and then Water St. When you spot the marina on your right, opposite Pearl St., pull in. Scanning the waterfront can be good for waterbirds, while the trail that runs south from the main parking lot is worth a check for waterbirds along the lake, if you have time. You might see the odd Caspian Tern in summer, and this spot can be decent for songbirds in spring and fall.

Continue north along Water St. and stay with it as it becomes Cumberland St. North, keeping an eye on the large grain elevators on your right (east) for Gyrfalcons. They like to hang out around the grain elevators as their prey, Rock Pigeons, are abundant here year-round. The best time for Gyrs is generally from mid-November to late March and this is the most reliable and accessible location in Ontario for the species. All three colour morphs have been seen here; however, the grey and brown morphs are most common.

Access Boulevard Lake by turning north (left) onto Gibson St., which will quickly turn into Lyon Blvd. West. Several parking areas are located on the west side of the lake and will be easy to see. The ground to your left (west) can be good in early spring and fall for geese, including rarer Ross's and Greater White-fronted, while to your right (east) is Boulevard Lake and a series of trails that can be good for passerines in migration.

Once you've had your fill of the city of Thunder Bay, it's likely time to head half an hour out of town to the Sibley Peninsula, which forms the other side of Thunder Bay Harbour. Go north on the Trans-Canada Hwy. (Hwy. 17) for about 50 km (31 mi.) and exit onto Hwy. 587 towards Pass Lake. The habitat here is markedly boreal, with typical species such as Black-backed Woodpecker, Spruce Grouse, and Boreal Chickadee present in any suitable conifer stands alongside the highway. While driving through the bush, pay attention to any clearings, as these can be good for owls, such as Great Grays, particularly in late fall and early winter. These areas can also be good for vagrant songbirds, like the Western Meadowlarks that have shown up occasionally in warmer months.

Sleeping Giant Provincial Park begins about 14 km (8.7 mi.) from Hwy. 17 and covers most of the peninsula. To access any of the trails within the park or to camp here, you'll be required to pay a small fee. Gatehouses are located at all of the campgrounds. Throughout the park are over 100 km (60 mi.) of hiking trails that vary in difficulty and length and that provide a good sense of the boreal-mixedwoods habitat. White-throated Sparrow, Hermit Thrush, Yellow-bellied Sapsucker, and Blue-headed Vireo, as well as a great variety of warblers, are common here in the breeding season. Wet conifer areas can be good for Olive-sided Flycatchers, while keeping an ear out for flyover finches can pay off at any time of year, as crossbills are highly nomadic and both species can be seen here.

At the very end of Hwy. 587 is the small lakeside village of Silver Islet (37 km/23 mi. from Hwy. 17). Silver Islet is worth a look at any time of year and has had its fair share of vagrants and unusual species over the years. Walking through the village is your best bet, checking the vacant lots and roadside gardens for odd species lurking about. When we bird the town in spring, we really get the sense that anything could be around the next corner. In summer, Common Terns and

Double-crested Cormorants are a common sight offshore. If you have access to a boat, you can launch here to go to TCBO, which is less than 10 km (6 mi.) away, or you can hike there along the Kabeyun Trail. To get to the trailhead, go back up Hwy. 587 for a kilometre north. The hike is quite strenuous and we'd recommend doing it only if you're in good physical shape and have lots of time, as it takes the better part of a day at a leisurely pace (it's not a spur-of-the-moment sort of thing!). If you decide to make the trek out to TCBO, it will be well worth it. Birding can be spectacular here in migration, with astounding numbers of passerines and waterbirds under the right conditions.

GETTING THERE

Thunder Bay is easily accessed by car along Hwy. 17 or by air from Toronto. The city offers a full range of accommodations, restaurants, and car rentals for visiting birders. Driving to Thunder Bay from Toronto takes a long time, generally between 15 and 24 hours. Flying from Toronto is about 1.5 hours.

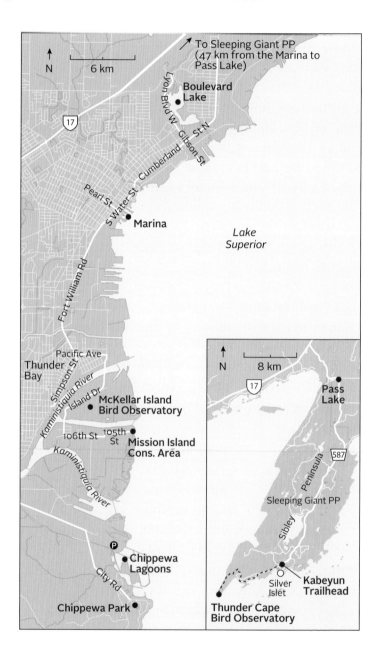

N 6 km

To Sleeping Giant PP
(47 km from the Marina to
Pass Lake)

Lyon Blvd W

Gibson St

St N

Boulevard
Lake

17

Pearl St

S Water St

Cumberland

Marina

Lake
Superior

Fort William Rd

Thunder
Bay

Pacific Ave

Simpson St

Kaministiquia River

Island Dr

McKellar Island
Bird Observatory

106th St

105th
St

Mission Island
Cons. Area

Kaministiquia River

Chippewa
Lagoons

City Rd

Chippewa Park

N 8 km

17

Pass
Lake

587

Sibley Peninsula

Sleeping Giant PP

Silver
Islet

Kabeyun
Trailhead

Thunder Cape
Bird Observatory

30
RAINY RIVER

OVERVIEW

Located along the border with Manitoba and Minnesota, the town of Rainy River and the surrounding area are home to more prairie and western bird species than you'll know what to do with. The Rainy River area lies just south of the Canadian Shield, in a region dominated by agriculture and speckled by stands of regenerating aspen and low-lying peatlands. The shores of Lake of the Woods and Rainy River are bordered by fairly rich deciduous forest, dominated in areas by Bur Oak. As a result of the varied habitats, the area provides birders a chance to see species found reliably nowhere else in the province, alongside a huge selection of other species.

Given the region's distance from many of the urban areas in the south, few birders regularly cover this area. Those who do, however, are rewarded with Black-billed Magpies, thousands of summering Franklin's Gulls, and breeding species including Western Meadowlarks, Marbled Godwits, Yellow-headed Blackbirds, and American White Pelicans. While the area is known for its prairie and western affinities, it's also a great place to get your dose of boreal breeding species, with Connecticut Warbler, Great Gray Owl, Spruce Grouse, and more. To top it off, there's an interesting southern element that includes species like Yellow-throated Vireo, Red-bellied Woodpecker, and Purple Martin.

On our first trip here, Mike had just reminded our family that we should look closely at any gulls because we "could" find a Franklin's Gull among any flock of gulls we might encounter. We stopped and scanned a field with a flock, and to our amazement every single gull we saw was a Franklin's. Our amazement, however, was not unusual among southern Ontario birders who arrive at Rainy River. The birdlife here is hugely different from anywhere else in the province, due to long, dry winters characteristic of the Prairie provinces and surprisingly warm summers ushered in by weather systems moving north from the Gulf Coast. Lake of the Woods, Ontario's sixth-largest lake, which borders the area, also contributes to the unique climate.

The Ontario Field Ornithologists lead an annual field trip here in late May and early June, and this is a great time to come for the region's breeding specialties. Both spring and fall can be fantastic too, netting many of the western specialties. While winter is birded much less, it can still produce interesting results.

While in the Rainy River area, you have a chance at finding a Great Gray Owl at any time of year. Search at dusk on the edges of wetlands or overgrown fields.

BRANDON HOLDEN

BIRDING STRATEGY

As is typical in northern Ontario, you'll need to cover a fairly large chunk of real estate; however, the Rainy River area provides a great variety of habitats and ultimately a high diversity of birds. We like to work our way from east to west when birding the area.

Starting at the intersection of Hwys. 11 and 619 in the hamlet of Pinewood, approximately 19 km (12 mi.) east of Rainy River, head north on Hwy. 619. After 4 km (2.5 mi.) you'll drive into Spruce Islands Provincial Park, a huge tamarack bog that has essentially every boreal species you could want in northern Ontario. Here you'll find Connecticut Warblers, Olive-sided Flycatchers, Great Gray Owls, both Black-backed and American Three-toed Woodpeckers, and Spruce Grouse to boot! The bog extends for close to 9 km (5.6 mi.), so stopping frequently along this stretch of road should yield your targets. Visiting in early June is best; however, some of the residents (e.g., woodpeckers, owls, and grouse) will be here year-round.

From here, head back along Hwy. 11 towards Rainy River and you'll quickly get into open, agricultural habitats. At the intersection with Worthington Rd. 3 (6.5 km/4 mi. east of Rainy River), turn onto this road and drive north to Byrnes Rd. (1.9 km/1.2 mi.). This short stretch can be good for Marbled Godwit. Listen for their very loud *kerreck* calls; under calm conditions you can hear them from over a kilometre away. When they aren't calling, however, they can be tricky to find.

Turn around here and head back towards Hwy. 11, continuing south on Worthington Rd. 3 one concession before turning west (right) onto Colonization Rd. Watch for Upland Sandpiper, Western Meadowlark, LeConte's Sparrow, Black-billed Magpie, and Marbled Godwit in this stretch of road. Brewer's Blackbird should be abundant, and keep an eye on the sky for overhead American White Pelicans. Continue west on Colonization Rd. to the T-junction with Worthington Rd. 1, watching for Red-headed Woodpeckers. (In fact, any area along the river can have them.) Turn north (right) onto Worthington Rd. 1 here and follow it to Hwy. 11. Take the highway west (left) to the town of Rainy River.

Once in Rainy River, check any vacant lots for Harris's Sparrow in migration. This species can be fairly common, with days of over 20 individuals not being uncommon. The waterfront is worth checking too; when the river is open, Common Goldeneyes, Pied-billed Grebes, and Double-crested Cormorants are frequently seen, while Purple Martins are present from mid-May through mid-August. From town, drive north on Government Rd. to 2nd Ave. and turn left (west). Look for the sewage lagoons at the end of the road and park at the gate. Walking around the sewage lagoons can be great, with breeding records of Eared Grebe, hundreds of northbound Wilson's Phalaropes annually during spring migration (the highest numbers in Ontario occur here), scattered Red-necked Phalaropes and Marbled Godwits, and, recently, rarities like Cinnamon Teal. In late May and from mid-July through early September the lagoons can have migrant shorebirds, with Stilt and Baird's Sandpipers being fairly regular, if there are exposed mud flats.

Once you've seen enough of the sewage lagoons, continue north on Government Rd. and then Hwy. 600 for a

One of many "prairie" bird species in the Rainy River area, Sharp-tailed Grouse are almost certain to turn up while you drive the roads through the region's agricultural areas. In spring, you may be treated to displaying males at their breeding leks. MARK PECK

total distance of 9.5 km (5.9 mi.) to the intersection of Wilson Creek Rd. Hwy. 600 between Government Rd. and Wilson Creek Rd. can be good for Black-billed Magpies. Following Wilson Creek Rd. west, check the agricultural fields, stopping regularly to watch and listen for LeConte's Sparrow, Sharp-tailed Grouse, and Sedge Wren in summer. In spring and fall, you might see flocks of sparrows and longspurs. In wet years, Yellow Rails and Nelson's Sparrows can also be present. Smith's Longspurs probably occur here in mid-April and late September but haven't yet been recorded, so keep a keen eye out during migration. The conifer areas along the road have had Great Gray Owls (dusk and dawn are generally the best times to look for this species), while Connecticut Warblers can be found in the aspen stands in early summer.

Continuing west on Wilson Creek Rd., the road will curve to the north and turn into River Rd. This area has had Red-bellied Woodpeckers in recent years, as they're quickly becoming established. The wooded areas along the river have some of the most northerly breeding populations of Yellow-throated Vireo and Eastern Whip-poor-will in the province, while uncommon breeders for the area include White-breasted Nuthatch. After about 4 km (2.5 mi.), River Rd. will make a series of 90-degree turns; stay on this road until you come to Fred's Rd. and turn left. Fred's Rd. dead-ends after about a kilometre; park here and walk out to the marsh. Remember to bring rubber boots—it can be particularly wet in spring and early summer. Outside of the Hudson Bay Lowlands, this area has consistently been the best location for breeding Yellow Rails. They should be present in wet years but mostly absent in dry years, while LeConte's and

Nelson's Sparrows (rare) and Sedge Wren are also possible. Short-eared Owls are also possible, as the marsh typically supports a few pairs.

Continuing from Fred's Marsh, take River Rd. east to Hwy. 600. Follow the highway north to the intersection with Budreau's Rd. and Fishery Rd. Harris Hill Resort is north of this intersection and has some feeders that can be productive, particularly for Yellow-headed Blackbirds during migration. The resort offers cabins and campsites, and visiting birders can also arrange with the resort to rent boats or be dropped off at Windy Point, which lies 2 km (1.4 mi.) to the north. Windy Point has had breeding Piping Plovers, though not reliably in recent years, and also hosts a fairly large nesting colony of Yellow-headed Blackbirds. The shoreline can have migrant shorebirds from mid-May to early June and again from mid-July to mid-September, while American White Pelicans and Franklin's Gulls (mid-June to the end of August) can be present in abundance. If you have the time and are adventurous, inquire at the resort about renting a boat and travelling to Sable Island. The island has also had nesting Piping Plovers and can support impressive numbers of loafing waterbirds. It has hosted several rarities over the years, despite having very little birding coverage.

Back at the resort, travel south to Hwy. 600 and head west (right) on Budreau's Rd. This road will dead-end at the shore of Lake of the Woods after 4 km (2.5 mi.). Anywhere along the road can be good for migrant songbirds, especially right at the end. The dead end also provides a good vantage point to scan the lake for waterbirds, such as American White Pelicans and Common Terns.

GETTING THERE

Plan to spend some time and money getting to Rainy River. Unless you're on an extended road trip, consider flying to Thunder Bay or Winnipeg and renting a car. It's a five-hour drive from Thunder Bay or a three-hour ride from Winnipeg along Hwy. 11 (the same Hwy. 11 that originates in Toronto). There is also an airport and rental car service in Fort Frances, just an hour from Rainy River, but that town has fewer flight connections to major centres.

The town of Rainy River has some basic restaurants and a motel. Just across the border in Minnesota is the town of Baudette, which has several stores and amenities that Rainy River doesn't offer, if you need more choice. Remember to bring your passport if you plan to cross the border.

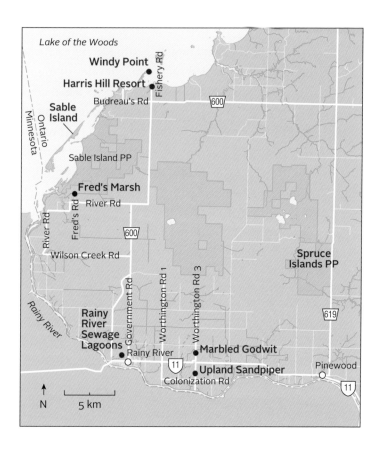

Lake of the Woods

Windy Point

Harris Hill Resort

Fishery Rd

Budreau's Rd

600

Sable
Island

Ontario
Minnesota

Sable Island PP

Fred's Marsh

Fred's Rd

River Rd

River Rd

600

Wilson Creek Rd

Spruce
Islands PP

Rainy River

Government Rd

Worthington Rd 1

Worthington Rd 3

619

Rainy
River
Sewage
Lagoons

Rainy River

Marbled Godwit

11

Upland Sandpiper

Pinewood

Colonization Rd

11

↑
N

5 km

ACKNOWLEDGEMENTS

THE GREAT THING about birding is that fellow birders are always so eager to share information with one another. Throughout our lives we have been so very fortunate to bird with many great people, all of whom have shared their personal stories, experiences, and tips without hesitation. Without you, our birding would be much duller and so would the contents of this book.

We'd particularly like to thank the photographers and regional experts who graciously reviewed individual chapters or provided site-specific information: Jody Allair, David Bree, Steve Charbonneau, Barb Charlton, Graeme Gibson (the Younger), Jeremy Hatt, Tyler Hoar, Brandon Holden, Sean Jenniskens, Stu Mackenzie, Dan MacNeal, Doug McRae, Nathan Miller, Gavin Platt, Paul Prior, David Pryor, Mark Read, Kory Renaud, Ron Ridout, Jon Ruddy, Rick Stronks, Don Sutherland, Ron Tozer, and Hazel Wheeler—our sincere apologies

ACKNOWLEDGEMENTS

if we have forgotten anyone. We'd also like to thank Dick and Russell Cannings for their idea on this series and Rob Sanders and the wonderful staff at Greystone for helping pull this book off. Ken also thanks the owners of Natural Resource Solutions Inc., David Stephenson and Elaine Gosnell, for their encouragement and willingness to support him in this endeavour.

Last, but certainly not least, our families deserve huge thanks as they have accompanied us on countless birding trips and supported us in the writing of the book.

To everyone reading, we wish you great birding ahead.

ABOUT THE AUTHORS

KENNETH BURRELL is a lifelong birder and naturalist. He is an active member of the Ontario Field Ornithologists and volunteers extensively with eBird and other not-for-profit organizations devoted to the study and conservation of birds. He also operates a guiding service—Burrell Birding—with his brother Mike. He holds a Bachelor and Master of Environmental Studies from the University of Waterloo and works as a biological consultant with Natural Resource Solutions Inc. Ken lives in Waterloo with his partner, Lillian.

MICHAEL BURRELL has been birding with his parents and three siblings since he was old enough to hold a pair of binoculars. He holds a Bachelor of Science from Trent University and a Master of Science from the University of Toronto and has conducted fieldwork around the province with private industry, Bird Studies Canada, and the Ontario Ministry of Natural Resources and Forestry, while running a guiding service—Burrell Birding—with his brother Ken. Mike lives in Peterborough with his wife, Erica, and daughter, Abigail.

INDEX

Pipit: American, 241; Sprague's, 248
Pittaway, Ron, 158, 166
Plover: Black-bellied, 20, 32, 35, 40,
122, 170, 241; Common Ringed,
145; at Lake St. Clair, 42; Lesser
Sand-, 175; Piping, 80, 87, 143, *148,*
150, 151, 154, 262; Semipalmated,
35, 122, 185; Snowy, 95; Wilson's,
143
Point Edward, 61
Point Pelee National Park: overview,
23–26; birding strategy, 26–29;
getting there, 29–30
Point Petre, 188
Port Bruce, 86, 89
Port Burwell, 84, 86–87, 89. *See also*
Port Stanley to Port Burwell
Port Credit, 133
Port Rowan. *See* Long Point
Port Stanley Sewage Lagoons,
84–85
Port Stanley to Port Burwell:
overview, 83–84; birding strategy,
84–87; getting there, 88–89
Prairie Smoke Alvar, 161
Presqu'ile Provincial Park: overview,
175–77; birding strategy, 177–80;
getting there, 180–81
Prince Edward County south shore:
overview, 183–84; birding strategy,
184–89; getting there, 189–90
Prince Edward Point Bird
Observatory, 186
Prince Edward Point National
Wildlife Area, 185–86
Ptarmigan, Willow, 145
Puffin, Atlantic, 223

Queenston, 104–6

Rail: at Hillman Marsh, 32; at
Long Point, 95; at Marshlands
Conservation Area, 212
Rail, specific species: King, 34, 36, 39,
42, 44, 48, 51, 96, 180; Virginia, 44,

54, 60, 79, 96, 153, 160, 234;
Yellow, 160, 232, 234, 242,
243, 261
Rainy River: overview, 255–56;
birding strategy, 258–59, 261–62;
getting there, 263–64
Rattray Marsh Conservation Area,
132–33
Raven, Common, 241
Razorbill, 104
Redhead, 11, 34, 45, 50, 54, *59,* 62,
107, 176, 177, 205, 210, 214
Redpoll: Common, 243; Hoary,
243; at Lac Deschênes, 219; at
Moosonee, 243; at Thunder
Bay, 248
Redstart, American, 26, 76,
79, *142*
Ridout, Ron, 92–93
Ring-necked Duck, 70, 212, 226
Robin, American, 186
Rondeau Provincial Park: overview,
47–48, 50; birding strategy, 50–55;
getting there, 55–56
Ruddy Duck, 20, 42, 60, 85, 122
Ruff, 35

Sandbanks Provincial Park, 189
Sand Beach Wetlands Conservation
Area, 203, 204–5
Sanderling, 85
Sandpiper: Baird's, 55, 219, 259;
Buff-breasted, 55; Curlew, 35;
Least, 122, 133; Pectoral, 72;
Purple, 34, 107, 114, 131, 135, *174,*
180, 188, 218; Semipalmated, 122,
133, 243; Solitary, 133; Stilt, 219,
259; Upland, *74,* 76, 78, 161, 185,
188, 192, 197, 202, 259; White-
rumped, 55, 243
Sapsucker, Yellow-bellied, 252
Sarnia: overview, 57–58; birding
strategy, 58, 60–63; getting
there, 63–64
Sauble Beach, 80